Applications of an Analytic Framework on Using Public Opinion Data for Solving Intelligence Problems

PROCEEDINGS OF A WORKSHOP

Linda Casola, *Rapporteur*

Board on Behavioral, Cognitive, and Sensory Sciences

Division of Behavioral and Social Sciences and Education

The National Academies of
SCIENCES · ENGINEERING · MEDICINE

THE NATIONAL ACADEMIES PRESS
Washington, DC
www.nap.edu

THE NATIONAL ACADEMIES PRESS   500 Fifth Street, NW   Washington, DC 20001

This activity was supported by contracts between the National Academy of Sciences and the United States Government. Support for the work of the Board on Behavioral, Cognitive, and Sensory Sciences is provided primarily by a grant from the National Science Foundation (Award No. BCS-1729167). Any opinions, findings, conclusions, or recommendations expressed in this publication do not necessarily reflect the views of any organization or agency that provided support for the project.

International Standard Book Number-13: 978-0-309-68801-7
International Standard Book Number-10: 0-309-68801-9
Digital Object Identifier: https://doi.org/10.17226/26548

Additional copies of this publication are available from the National Academies Press, 500 Fifth Street, NW, Keck 360, Washington, DC 20001; (800) 624-6242 or (202) 334-3313; http://www.nap.edu.

Copyright 2022 by the National Academy of Sciences. All rights reserved.

Printed in the United States of America

Suggested citation: National Academies of Sciences, Engineering, and Medicine. (2022). *Applications of an Analytic Framework on Using Public Opinion Data for Solving Intelligence Problems: Proceedings of a Workshop.* Washington, DC: The National Academies Press. https:// doi.org/10.17226/26548.

The National Academies of
SCIENCES · ENGINEERING · MEDICINE

The **National Academy of Sciences** was established in 1863 by an Act of Congress, signed by President Lincoln, as a private, nongovernmental institution to advise the nation on issues related to science and technology. Members are elected by their peers for outstanding contributions to research. Dr. Marcia McNutt is president.

The **National Academy of Engineering** was established in 1964 under the charter of the National Academy of Sciences to bring the practices of engineering to advising the nation. Members are elected by their peers for extraordinary contributions to engineering. Dr. John L. Anderson is president.

The **National Academy of Medicine** (formerly the Institute of Medicine) was established in 1970 under the charter of the National Academy of Sciences to advise the nation on medical and health issues. Members are elected by their peers for distinguished contributions to medicine and health. Dr. Victor J. Dzau is president.

The three Academies work together as the **National Academies of Sciences, Engineering, and Medicine** to provide independent, objective analysis and advice to the nation and conduct other activities to solve complex problems and inform public policy decisions. The National Academies also encourage education and research, recognize outstanding contributions to knowledge, and increase public understanding in matters of science, engineering, and medicine.

Learn more about the National Academies of Sciences, Engineering, and Medicine at **www.nationalacademies.org**.

The National Academies of
SCIENCES · ENGINEERING · MEDICINE

Consensus Study Reports published by the National Academies of Sciences, Engineering, and Medicine document the evidence-based consensus on the study's statement of task by an authoring committee of experts. Reports typically include findings, conclusions, and recommendations based on information gathered by the committee and the committee's deliberations. Each report has been subjected to a rigorous and independent peer-review process and it represents the position of the National Academies on the statement of task.

Proceedings published by the National Academies of Sciences, Engineering, and Medicine chronicle the presentations and discussions at a workshop, symposium, or other event convened by the National Academies. The statements and opinions contained in proceedings are those of the participants and are not endorsed by other participants, the planning committee, or the National Academies.

For information about other products and activities of the National Academies, please visit www.nationalacademies.org/about/whatwedo.

PLANNING COMMITTEE ON MEASUREMENT AND ANALYSIS OF PUBLIC OPINION: A WORKSHOP ON THE ANALYTIC FRAMEWORK AND ITS APPLICATIONS

CHARLES LAU (*Chair*), RTI International
JAMES N. DRUCKMAN, Northwestern University
COURTNEY KENNEDY, Pew Research Center
SCOTT E. PAGE, University of Michigan

Staff

DYLAN THOMAS REBSTOCK, *Project Director*
TINA M. WINTERS, *Associate Program Officer*
EMMA FINE, *Associate Program Officer*
JACQUELINE COLE, *Senior Program Assistant*
BARBARA A. WANCHISEN, *Senior Advisor for Behavioral Sciences*
SAMANTHA CHAO, *Associate Executive Director Extension, National Research Council Programs*

Acknowledgments

This Proceedings of a Workshop was reviewed in draft form by individuals chosen for their diverse perspectives and technical expertise. The purpose of this independent review is to provide candid and critical comments that will assist the National Academies of Sciences, Engineering, and Medicine in making each published proceedings as sound as possible and to ensure that it meets the institutional standards for quality, objectivity, evidence, and responsiveness to the charge. The review comments and draft manuscript remain confidential to protect the integrity of the process.

We thank the following individual for their review of this proceedings: David Tully, U.S. Department of State. We also thank staff member Ryan Murphy for reading and providing helpful comments on this manuscript.

Although the reviewers listed above provided many constructive comments and suggestions, they were not asked to endorse the content of the proceedings, nor did they see the final draft before its release. The review of this proceedings was overseen by Jonathan D. Moreno, Department of Medical Ethics and Health Policy, University of Pennsylvania. He was responsible for making certain that an independent examination of this proceedings was carried out in accordance with standards of the National Academies and that all review comments were carefully considered. Responsibility for the final content rests entirely with the rapporteur and the National Academies.

The National Academies' staff and the workshop planning committee also express their gratitude to the National Academies' Conference Management team members for their dedication to ensuring a logistically smooth workshop.

Contents

INTRODUCTION 1

1 PUBLIC OPINION DATA AND THE *ANALYTIC FRAMEWORK* 5

2 HYPOTHETICAL APPLICATIONS OF THE *ANALYTIC FRAMEWORK* 21

3 LESSONS LEARNED AND FUTURE PATHWAYS 47

REFERENCES 53

APPENDIXES
A Workshop Agenda 55
B Biographical Information for Workshop Participants 63

Introduction

Measuring and analyzing public opinion comes with tremendous challenges, as evidenced by recent struggles to predict election outcomes and to anticipate mass mobilizations. The National Academies of Sciences, Engineering, and Medicine publication *Measurement and Analysis of Public Opinion: An Analytic Framework* (hereafter referred to as the *Analytic Framework*) presents in-depth information from experts on how to collect and glean insights from public opinion data, particularly in conditions where contextual issues call for applying caveats to those data (NASEM, 2022). The *Analytic Framework* is designed specifically to help intelligence community (IC) analysts apply insights from the social and behavioral sciences on state-of-the-art approaches to analyze public attitudes in non-Western populations.

Sponsored by the IC, the National Academies' Board on Behavioral, Cognitive, and Sensory Sciences hosted a 2-day hybrid workshop on March 8–9, 2022, to present the *Analytic Framework* and to demonstrate its application across a series of hypothetical scenarios that might arise for an intelligence analyst tasked with summarizing public attitudes to inform a policy decision (see Box I-1 for the workshop's Statement of Task and Appendix A for the workshop agenda). Workshop participants explored cutting-edge methods for using large-scale data as well as cultural and ethical considerations for the collection and use of public opinion data.

> **BOX I-1**
> **Statement of Task**
>
> A planning committee of the National Academies of Science, Engineering and Medicine will plan and execute a 2-day, public workshop to discuss the highlights and practical aspects from a project on the development of an analytic framework designed to help Intelligence Community (IC) analysts apply insights from the social and behavioral sciences to better inform policy makers. The workshop will address current methods for using public opinion data to inform international affairs, how analysts can best use that knowledge, and how analysts can best combine and communicate their insights to the policy community. The workshop will bring together IC analysts, experts overseeing the framework, and commissioned paper authors to discuss the development and use of the framework and possible lessons for future framework projects.

OPENING REMARKS

Charles Lau (co-lead expert contributor for the *Analytic Framework* and director of the International Survey Research Program at RTI International) described the work of intelligence analysts as particularly challenging: they are expected to evaluate disparate sources of information that are rarely designed to address the question at hand and that could be of varying levels of quality, and to provide recommendations to policy makers in extremely brief time frames. He invited workshop participants to consider how to apply the *Analytic Framework* to real-world situations as a means to best assist intelligence analysts in their day-to-day tasks.

The *Analytic Framework*

Lau explained that the *Analytic Framework* is not, for the most part, a prescriptive document; rather, it offers approaches to inform the work of intelligence analysts who are evaluating public opinion research in international contexts. It serves as a guide both for the collection of new data and the assessment of existing data, and is meant to be (1) rigorous, (2) helpful, and (3) suitable for a wide range of audiences. First, leading academic and applied research was produced and compiled for the *Analytic Framework* by an interdisciplinary panel of authors and expert contributors. Second, because intelligence analysts encounter different challenges each day, the *Analytic Framework* offers both a broad set of tools that apply for various intelligence analysts in different regions and contexts as well as focused checklists to structure tasks. Third, to address the varied levels of experience with public opinion research throughout the IC, the *Analytic*

Framework is presented in three layers—the foundational layer includes four commissioned academic papers, the synthesis layer provides a high-level summary of these academic papers, and a graphic layer illustrates key messages about relevant phases of data collection and analysis.

Workshop Goals

Lau presented four goals for the 2-day workshop: (1) provide an overview of the *Analytic Framework's* components—the foundational papers, the synthesis, and the graphic depiction of the phases involved in collecting and analyzing public opinion data; (2) examine key messages in the *Analytic Framework* and discuss what it does and does not do; (3) explore cultural and ethical considerations in the collection and use of public opinion data; and (4) engage in several exercises applying the *Analytic Framework* to theoretical scenarios and address intelligence analysts' questions about its application.

ORGANIZATION OF THIS PROCEEDINGS

Chapter 1 describes the role of public opinion in intelligence analysis, with particular emphasis on the challenges that analysts face amidst a continually evolving landscape. Key ethical and cultural considerations for the use of public opinion data are discussed, and a more detailed overview of the goals for, structure of, and responses to the *Analytic Framework* is provided. Chapter 2 presents four hypothetical scenarios and the ensuing conversations about how an intelligence analyst could use the *Analytic Framework* to approach them. Chapter 3 summarizes insights from the *Analytic Framework* and the workshop, and highlights areas for future discussion.

This proceedings document has been prepared by the workshop rapporteur as a factual summary of what occurred at the workshop. The workshop planning committee's role was limited to organizing and convening the workshop (see Appendix B for biographical sketches of the planning committee members, expert contributors, authors, and other workshop participants). The views contained in the proceedings are those of individual workshop participants and do not necessarily represent the views of all workshop participants, the planning committee, or the National Academies.

1

Public Opinion Data and the *Analytic Framework*

HISTORY AND CURRENT STATUS OF PUBLIC OPINION RESEARCH IN THE INTELLIGENCE COMMUNITY

Regina Faranda (director of the Office of Opinion Research at the U.S. Department of State) explained that public opinion has played an important role in the intelligence analysis that supports U.S. policy since 1948. The Office of Opinion Research has a mandate to ensure that the U.S. government is aware of how the global public thinks and how that affects U.S. interests. To fulfill this mandate, she continued, it is imperative that intelligence analysts keep pace with current trends in public opinion research methods.

Faranda shared an example of the intelligence community's (IC's) effective use of public opinion research in the identification of macrotrends, which could help predict when conditions are most suitable for protests. Relevant data collection could include public views of the economy, politics, food insecurity, local leaders, and corruption. Although these factors alone might not provoke a protest, public opinion research offers insight into individual drivers of protest alongside regional context to create better predictions. Social science research is most useful when understood within a regional or national context. She mentioned that protest has become a normalized form of expression in certain countries; for example, in some African nations, people who have experienced bribery are more likely to support anticorruption protests. Public opinion research can also help identify redlines for the public in the form of constitutional revision, egregious corruption, or attempts to circumvent term limits.

CHALLENGES FOR INTELLIGENCE ANALYSTS IN A CONTINUALLY EVOLVING LANDSCAPE

Faranda described the rapidly changing landscape within which intelligence analysts work; for example, the evolution of machine learning and the tools for data modeling, the increased use of social media, and the broad access to quick and inexpensive communication have created an inflection point for public opinion research. She emphasized that the significance of public opinion analysis is unlikely to diminish, and the use of empirical research is likely to increase. However, as public opinion research becomes exponentially more sophisticated in the United States, the quality of opinion research abroad varies widely and often lags behind that of the United States, creating challenges for drawing on the findings from international survey research to inform U.S. foreign policy. Further complicating this issue is the fact that policy readers have to be able to understand increasingly technical arguments. She asserted that the IC has a responsibility to make these arguments more relatable for its clients.

A representative from the IC championed the *Analytic Framework's* role in helping intelligence analysts leverage the most recent advances in social and behavioral sciences to complete their jobs, which vary from day to day and between individuals. She highlighted several differences between the work of analysts in the IC and experts in academia. Intelligence analysts

- diagnose a situation as it unfolds and look for the implications;
- react to events where they occur instead of developing their own lines of inquiry;
- generalize from findings that might not relate to the problem at hand and operate under significant ambiguity;
- have customers who are generalists, not experts, who are responsible for making decisions about difficult real-world problems; and
- assess the meaning of complex developments under significant time pressure and present their findings concisely to busy policy makers.

A representative from the IC remarked that the past decade of protests around the world has solidified for intelligence analysts and policy makers the importance of understanding public mood. However, with the widespread use of polling and the criticism of polling methods around the world (e.g., in the context of U.S. elections) as well as the fact that, as Faranda mentioned, international polling methods often lag (or are perceived to lag) behind those of the United States, she noted that it can be difficult for intelligence analysts to communicate assessments about foreign publics to U.S. policy makers. Analysts make judgments and present their best insights in short time frames. Furthermore, products from the

IC generally reflect the coordinated views of several stakeholders instead of a single author. Highly skilled analysts often reach varied conclusions about the same phenomenon owing to the differences in their quantitative, qualitative, and statistical training and to constraints on data availability, data access, and time. The IC is challenged to ensure that it rigorously synthesizes and clearly communicates these insights across methodological divides. She asserted that the *Analytic Framework* could help intelligence analysts select and apply the best methods to derive judgments; synthesize perspectives; and provide concise, persuasive, and timely insights about what they think, what they know, and how they know it to diverse customers who lack the time and expertise to discuss the underlying analytical methodology.

OVERVIEW OF THE *ANALYTIC FRAMEWORK*

Elizabeth Zechmeister (co-lead expert contributor for the *Analytic Framework*, and Cornelius Vanderbilt Professor of Political Science and director of the Latin American Public Opinion Project at Vanderbilt University) elaborated on the heterogeneity in (1) intelligence analysts' prior training and experience with survey methodology; (2) the types of questions being explored by intelligence analysts and the ways that survey data intersect with them; and (3) the types of data that are available or could be generated to make an assessment. Recognition of this heterogeneity played an important role in the creation of the multilayered *Analytic Framework* (NASEM, 2022), which was generated with the contributions of an advisory panel of 12 experts in survey and social science research methods; 5 subject-matter experts who authored four commissioned papers; a technical writer who wrote the synthesis; National Academies of Sciences, Engineering, and Medicine staff; and liaisons from the IC. Because public opinion data are a critical input into intelligence analysts' assessments of attitudes in foreign populations, she continued, the following question guided the work of the expert contributors to and authors of the *Analytic Framework*: how can the IC analyze, make inferences from, and present public opinion data in ways that align with best practices, while acknowledging that these data are not always perfect or complete?

Zechmeister emphasized that the *Analytic Framework* is not designed to offer direct answers to research questions or a set of preset instructions for every situation. Instead, it empowers intelligence analysts to conduct systematic evaluations guided by best practices. In essence, the analyst has three tasks: make an estimate about public attitudes and/or opinions; use available techniques to make that estimate as precise as possible; and make an assessment about the degree of certainty or uncertainty of that estimate. She remarked that the *Analytic Framework* introduces intelligence analysts to the appropriate ways to use and evaluate public opinion data, with careful attention to the design and interpretation of attitudinal data, the adjustment of inferences to communicate likely bias and uncertainty, the use of alternative data sources when appropriate, and the combination of insights from different data sources (i.e., triangulation).

Structure of the *Analytic Framework*

Zechmeister and Charles Lau (co-lead expert contributor for the *Analytic Framework* and director of the International Survey Research Program at RTI International) outlined the structure of the *Analytic Framework*, which consists of a foundational layer, a synthesis layer, and a graphic layer.

Foundational Layer

Zechmeister noted that the foundational layer is targeted toward intelligence analysts with prior training and experience in survey methodology. It includes four white papers (summarized below), which contain detailed discussions of and citations to relevant academic work.

"Drawing Inferences from Public Opinion Surveys: Insights for Intelligence Reports," by René Bautista (associate director of the Methodology and Quantitative Social Sciences Department at NORC, University of Chicago), provides an overview of how survey methodologists evaluate data quality using two criteria: credibility and soundness. Credibility can be assessed by collecting contextual information about the survey's purpose, authenticity, and sponsorship, as well as the reputation of the survey firm, through the documentation that accompanies the data. A lack of available documentation indicates a lower level of credibility. Soundness considers the survey design features that can influence bias and error; for example, the nature of the sample (probability versus nonprobability); whether the sample represents the population of interest, sample coverage, item measurement (i.e., what the question was and how it was asked); response rates; and weights. Zechmeister pointed out that a higher survey participation rate is not always indicative of high quality or representativeness, and that if nonresponse to a particular question is high, respondents could be censoring answers to a sensitive question. Thus, the analyst could consider the following question: Is there evidence that participation in the survey is skewed in a way that the survey weights cannot overcome to make inferences about the population of interest? Bautista's paper presents a rating system that intelligence analysts can use to help assess about the quality of a dataset and to explain their level of confidence in the result to the customer: (1) "credible and sound"; (2) "partially credible, partially sound"; or (3) "not credible, not sound."

"Alternatives to Probability-based Surveys Representative of the General Population for Measuring Attitudes," by Ashley Amaya (senior survey methodologist at Pew Research Center), offers guidance on how to select and use nonprobability-based approaches to gather insight on public opinion. Zechmeister commented that although pure probability-based survey methods are the "gold standard," they are not always available or required to address particular research questions. Amaya's paper reveals that the selection of alternative methods depends on the question (e.g., assessment of the general population or a subgroup) and the priorities (e.g., timeliness, single-point precision, or across-time changes) of interest, and that nonprobability alternative sources can be evaluated for their strengths and weaknesses with the use of a 2×2 matrix: (1) designed data, which emerge from a systematic attempt to address a particular question, versus organic data, which emerge for another purpose but might still provide insight into public opinion; and (2) primary data (i.e., collected by the researcher) versus secondary data (i.e., collected by others). Alternative approaches include complex sample surveys, nonprobability surveys (e.g., an online survey for which participants are invited from a firm-maintained panel, often based on quotas for age, wealth, location, and gender), qualitative research, and social media data. Zechmeister mentioned that although online surveys might have coverage issues (e.g., lack of Internet access in certain countries), the data from those surveys could still be useful. The same principle applies to social media data, which are often noisy and biased but could help to uncover the context in which many in a population are functioning. Amaya's paper also highlights ethical considerations for alternatives to pure probability-based general population surveys.

"Ascertaining True Attitudes in Survey Research," by Kanisha Bond (assistant professor of political science at Binghamton University, State University of New York), defines "true attitudes" as "predispositions that are honestly held, and reflective of the respondent's sense of the real state of the world; true responses to attitude inquiries…are honestly communicated descriptions of those predispositions" (NASEM, 2022). Attitudes are difficult to measure because they are multidimensional; for example, survey results can include implicit/explicit attitudes, nonattitudes, strategic responses that mask true attitudes, partial attitudes, and nonresponses. Bond's paper emphasizes that the ethical and technical issues of measuring attitude are intertwined—ethics can affect the quality as well as the technical ability of a survey to reveal true attitudes (e.g., if participants experience harm during the data collection or fear retribution for their responses, they are unlikely to provide high-quality responses). Lau observed that unethical surveys can also lead intelligence analysts to make inaccurate recommendations to policy makers. Bond's paper describes eight challenges that arise when trying to measure true attitudes, especially in locations with high conflict:

1. Purposeful misrepresentation (a researcher deceives a respondent);
2. Power dynamics (respondents either answer the survey in favorable ways to please the sponsor or contribute false information to sabotage the survey);
3. Fragile or volatile contexts (being in a conflict area can alter attitudes);
4. Potential for direct harm (sensitive survey questions can cause trauma or create security risks for respondents);
5. Sensitive topics (respondents might underreport "socially undesirable" attitudes);
6. Time (people's attitudes change over time and in different environments);
7. Sampling and exposure (populations can be over-surveyed); and
8. Questionnaire type, question forms, and intercultural literacy.

Her paper assists intelligence analysts in identifying these challenges, connecting that understanding to the interpretation of data, and recognizing how policy recommendations could be affected. Understanding the data generation process helps an analyst assign bias to items and avoid presenting an inaccurate policy recommendation.

"Integrating Data Across Sources," by Josh Pasek (associate professor of communication and media and political science, faculty associate in the Center for Political Studies, and core faculty for the Michigan Institute for Data Science at the University of Michigan) and Sunghee Lee (research associate professor at the Institute for Social Research at the University of Michigan), offers guidance to intelligence analysts about how to apply multiple datasets to answer a question. Lau explained that combining datasets helps to better understand the flaws of those datasets and employ methods to correct them, and to enhance the quality of the policy recommendation. Pasek and Lee's paper defines data integration as "the process of taking multiple diverse streams of information and finding ways to use them jointly to make conclusions, reconcile their differences, and/or determine where they provide complementary or conflicting understandings" (NASEM, 2022). The paper emphasizes that before integrating data, intelligence analysts should understand the nature of the data and harmonize those data to confirm that integration and comparison are possible, using processes such as data cleaning, linking sample data with the population, addressing data missingness, generating a composite measure, and validating. Once the data have been harmonized and then combined, several techniques are available for data analysis and integration (e.g., ensemble methods).

Synthesis Layer

The second layer of the *Analytic Framework*, the synthesis layer, "Using Public Opinion Research to Answer an Intelligence Question," written by Rona Briere (independent contractor), presents the core components of the *Analytic Framework* in a way that is more accessible to intelligence analysts who do not have extensive training in or experience with survey methodology. Zechmeister described this layer as an "orientation to the fundamental ideas and best practices of public opinion research."

Graphic Layer

Zechmeister explained that the top layer of the *Analytic Framework* is a graphic that presents a decision tree with four iterative phases, which could be useful to guide the work on a time-sensitive task of an intelligence analyst who has either attended this workshop or has read the synthesis layer. During Phase 0, the analyst generates or is assigned a research question. In Phase 1, the analyst collects existing data and/or decides to collect new data, based on available resources, the question, and the time line. She emphasized how important it is for the analyst to consider whether the existing data represent the population of interest—the foundational layer of the *Analytic Framework* includes guidance on the use of alternative sources to strengthen inferences. Phase 2 provides an opportunity to analyze the data by conducting an ethics check, interpreting the results that can be generated with the data, and evaluating the quality of the data. Phase 3 serves to inform the inferences that the analyst has drawn and to build confidence in those inferences. The analyst iterates through this process, with consideration for aspects that could confirm, qualify, or contextualize the inferences (e.g., whether the population might self-censor on a certain type of question) (see Figure 1-1).

Responses to the *Analytic Framework*

A representative from the IC reiterated the challenges of bridging the gap between the IC and academia. However, the *Analytic Framework* helps shift the IC's focus away from answering narrow questions toward thinking more broadly and with more structure. She underscored a gap in the literature included in the *Analytic Framework*, which is a lack of information on the relationship between attitudes and behavior. She encouraged the experts to continue to share innovative methods with the IC as well as areas of uncertainty for which they have not yet identified the best route to address difficult questions.

Bautista expressed his hope that the *Analytic Framework* will expose analysts to strategies that they might not encounter in academic textbooks.

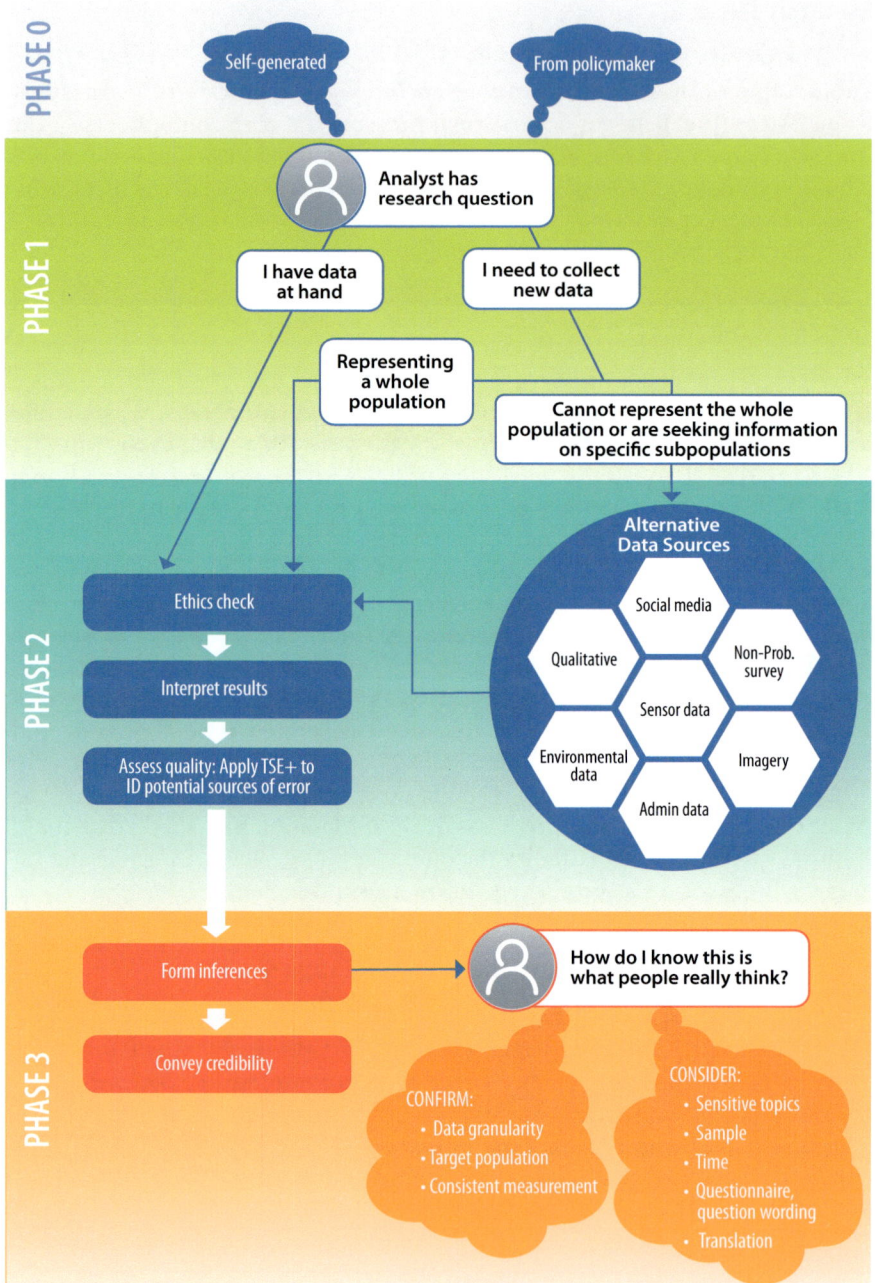

FIGURE 1-1 The *Analytic Framework's* graphic representation of a decision tree for public opinion data collection and analysis. SOURCE: NASEM (2022).

He emphasized the value of contextual elements (highlighted in his paper), which are critical in the overall assessment of any survey. Amaya commented that in addition to discussing nonprobability-based approaches, her paper describes several probability-based approaches for surveys with a purpose other than to measure the general population, and includes techniques that illuminate the best option. Her paper also presents an overview of the advantages and disadvantages of each alternative approach. She urged intelligence analysts to reflect on these strengths and weaknesses alongside the evaluative measures presented in Bautista's paper. It is critical to understand priorities before choosing a dataset. Because no dataset is perfect, she stressed that the best choice is the one that works for the analyst and their purpose. Pasek pointed out that combining datasets can lead to several possible outcomes and answers to a question, which can be both inspiring and discouraging. Although combining data will always be messy, he continued, identifying consistencies will provide strong support for inferences.

Bond emphasized that because technical and ethical approaches to understanding attitudes are intertwined, they have to be carefully balanced (in addition to weighing issues of robustness and precision in estimation). The question of whether a systematic ethical irregularity exists affects how well intelligence analysts can use data to infer what people think, and she indicated that further conversation about that issue would be beneficial. Faranda asserted that it is crucial to be attentive to the "people part of public opinion"—for example, questions have to be relevant and phrased in a way that people can access. Quoting anthropologist Cora Du Bois, Faranda said, "It behooves us to . . . use our new powers with judicious and constructive wisdom." Courtney Kennedy (expert contributor for the *Analytic Framework* and director of survey research at Pew Research Center) championed Faranda's advice never to lose focus of the people in the population of interest, especially as online data collection increases and more countries are surveyed online. She revealed that conducting online surveys makes it easier to lose touch with how people are reacting to questions, and suggested the development of best practices for how to test and ensure that online measurements are sound and resonate with the population.

ETHICAL AND CULTURAL CONSIDERATIONS IN THE COLLECTION AND USE OF PUBLIC OPINION DATA

Ethical Considerations

Zachariah Mampilly (expert contributor for the *Analytic Framework* and Marxe Endowed Chair of International Affairs at the Marxe School of Public and International Affairs, City University of New York) echoed Bond's assertion that the ethical and technical facets of public opinion research are intertwined: no inherent tradeoff between them exists, especially in the case of foreign policy. Unethical research practices undermine the quality of the research and could thus undermine foreign policy objectives. He encouraged workshop participants to read Bond's paper in the *Analytic Framework* as well as additional literature on the ethical issues that arise specifically in political violence–affected contexts (see ARC, n.d.; Arjona, Mampilly, and Pearlman, 2019).

Mampilly cited the Tuskegee experiment as an example of the long afterlife of unethical research (e.g., reluctance toward COVID-19 vaccinations among certain communities) and the need to be concerned about the victims of such unethical experimentation. Because the U.S. government distinguishes itself from its enemies in terms of its concern with ethical practices, he continued, ethics are not only a moral imperative but also an essential component of the identity of the United States.

Reflecting on the connection between academia and the IC, Mampilly remarked that their relationship is the closest it has been for decades. For example, after Vietnam, suspicions arose owing to the perception that academic researchers were being turned into "tools of the U.S. government." This perception began to change after 9/11, when cooperation between academia and the IC improved significantly. The level of collaboration between the two communities has continued to fluctuate over the course of administrations. Now, the nature of the relationship between academia and the IC is being reevaluated, and he described an opportunity for enhanced inquiry into ethical research between the two communities.

Bond explained that both challenges and opportunities arise in understanding true attitudes of a population as a result of the ethical and technical considerations for survey research. She also described the interconnected nature of those who conduct research and those who participate in research and noted that ensuring the security and safety of *all* individuals involved in survey research is critical. Because the "human core" (i.e., human ideals, beliefs, preferences, and political behaviors) is paramount, she continued, research should be conducted ethically and rigorously.

Bond commented that researchers should be attuned to systematic ethical irregularities. She stressed that the purpose of her paper is not to "make calls" for others about what constitutes an appropriate research process; instead, it provides general guidance about acceptable research practice and acceptable uses of human data. Various professional associations (e.g., the American Association for Public Opinion Research [AAPOR] and the American Political Science Association) have developed codes of ethics, but those do not replace the personal ethics of any intelligence analyst who is engaged with the research; the analyst plays just as important a role as the research subject in terms of ethical considerations. The more volatile the environment, she continued, the more opportunity for ethical irregularities to arise; the paper explores how to determine what respondents think based on their location in their complex security relationships. The concept of a "true attitude" emerges when asking whether something is "real" to the respondent; "Is what you are telling me what you believe?" is a complicated, yet universally human question. She suggested supporting individuals in their thoughts about and challenges in doing ethical work as well as raising awareness of context and the integration of that context into the work.

Cultural Considerations

Michele Gelfand (expert contributor for the *Analytic Framework;* John H. Scully Professor in Cross-Cultural Management and professor of organizational behavior, Stanford Graduate School of Business; and professor of psychology [by courtesy], School of Humanities and Sciences, Stanford University) explained that the realities that surround humans, like culture, tend to be taken for granted or misunderstood; people often do not realize how they are part of a culture or how they have been affected by cultural values and norms until they experience another culture. She emphasized that culture affects each stage of the research process.

Gelfand asserted that cross-cultural research poses several unique methodological issues. Research itself is a cultural process, and the result could be the introduction of several "extraneous variables" unrelated to the question of interest. Each of those variables can pose "rival hypotheses" for any differences identified across cultures; if these variables are not addressed, conclusions could be misleading. These rival hypotheses can be represented as a regression problem, $Y' = \tau_y + \Sigma k_i, + \varepsilon$, where k_i is any systematic variation other than τ that affects Y' (the prediction) (see Malpass, 1977). In other words, the sum of k_i's is the bias that affects the prediction. In unicultural research, she continued, researchers are implicitly aware of possible cultural k_i's that can bias results; within cross-cultural research, however, unknown cultural k_i's might not be measured or controlled, thus affecting interventions.

Gelfand emphasized that although constructs and measurements should be representative of the culture of interest, people often try unsuccessfully to transfer constructs and measurement developed in the United States into another cultural context. She explained that this use of "imposed etics"[1] is similar to comparing apples to oranges. She provided an example research question relating to whether organizational embeddedness, a U.S. construct,

---

[1] Merriam Webster defines "etic" as "of, relating to, or involving analysis of cultural phenomena from the perspective of one who does not participate in the culture being studied."

had a role in radical organizations in terms of predicting attitudes toward radicalization. Using techniques such as confirmatory factor analysis, the first step was to assess whether the construct represented the phenomenon in this particular context. She underscored the importance of equivalence of measurement—that is, whether items are relevant, similar across cultures, contaminated, or deficient. Because a technique such as confirmatory factor analysis could not address issues of deficiency in particular, it was necessary to conduct interviews and focus groups in the country of interest to better understand constructs and add items more relevant in that country's context. She suggested a "combined etic-emic[2] strategy" (Berry, 1969), in which a researcher begins with a particular cultural perspective; collects culture-specific (i.e., "emic") information from other countries; and incorporates this information to create a new "etic" so that the final construct is more representative across cultures. A relevant example is work on the U.S. construct of organizational citizenship behaviors (OCBs) in China (Farh et al., 1997). The researchers discovered that certain dimensions of OCBs were relevant in both cultures; others were relevant in the United States but not relevant in China; and still others were relevant in China but not relevant in the United States. She cautioned researchers about their constructs; what has developed to scale in the United States could be irrelevant, deficient, or contaminated in other contexts.

Gelfand asserted that methods for cross-cultural research should be appropriate, be replicable, have ample depth, and be ethically acceptable (see Gelfand et al., 2002; Hui and Triandis, 1985). She pointed out that triangulating multiple methods in cross-cultural research could enhance confidence in the results. Interviews and focus groups could offer great depth of information and emic perspectives, but problems could arise when cultural k_i's are added, thus misrepresenting attitudes. For instance, although an interviewer might be readily trusted in the United States, this is uncommon in other parts of the world, where more time is spent to develop trust. Furthermore, interviewer characteristics could differentially impact participants, the interview could prompt reactance (e.g., if payment is offered for participation), the format of the interview might be culturally inappropriate (e.g., a female interviewing a male), or the interview could lack standardization. To avoid the influence of cultural k_i's, she suggested developing a structured interview protocol, reviewing the content and structure with local collaborators and being prepared to make changes as needed, using local interviewers with characteristics similar to those of the participants, conducting a pre-interview/focus group to detect problems, and standardizing interviewers. Questionnaires are less expensive than

---

[2]Merriam Webster defines "emic" as "of, relating to, or involving analysis of cultural phenomena from the perspective of one who participates in the culture being studied."

other methods and allow for the relatively unobtrusive collection of significant amounts of data; however, differences in respondents' motivations to answer questions, differences in familiarity with materials, and problems with rating scales and response sets across cultures create challenges. She advised conducting extensive piloting, gathering input from local collaborators, using alternative scale formats, being cautious of using long surveys with complex language, and combining questionnaires with other methods to reveal convergence. Another key consideration in cross-cultural research is language. Although the right choice of language is not always obvious, it is important because it communicates the purpose of the study and can influence the results. She cautioned researchers to take care with accurate translation and backtranslation. Field or laboratory experiments can be useful in addressing causality and understanding implicit attitudes, but they can be obtrusive, lack context, create a differential understanding of the task and the motivation, and include manipulated variables with different strengths. She advocated for researchers to conduct multiple pilots and gather feedback from local collaborators, anticipate changes and revise as appropriate to reflect context, use local experimenters who have similarities to the participants, and use experimentation alongside other methods. Content analysis is an unobtrusive way to gather accounts of culture from documents. For example, linguistic dictionaries (Choi et al., 2022) can be created to better understand cultural constructs and underlying attitudes, and proverbs can be analyzed to understand how cultures view risk (Weber et al., 1998). She suggested that researchers invite local collaborators to identify appropriate documents, be cautious of noncomparable sources, and create a reliable coding manual in all cultures. Observations are also used in cross-cultural research, providing unobtrusive data and indicators that can be difficult to evaluate with other methods. She encouraged researchers to confirm that the situation sampling is appropriate, that participants in field experiments are standardized, and that ethics are considered within a local context. Ecological and historical databases provide a rich source of data to connect cultural dimensions but can be unreliable, she continued, and computational methods can aid in the study of cultural dynamics and the study of theories that are difficult to test in the field. She advocated for clear and carefully justified assumptions, understanding of the generalizability of results, and replication with other methods. Because cultural assumptions can affect choices made in the models, however, she reiterated the importance of working with local collaborators. Overarching concerns about analyzing data relate to cultural response sets, structural equivalence, and aggregation issues.

In summary, Gelfand reiterated that cross-cultural research is far more complicated than unicultural research, owing to the emphasis on the appropriateness, reliability, depth, and ethics of each method amidst a backdrop of cultural concerns. She reaffirmed the value of using pilots for tasks and instructions, being flexible to adjust, measuring and controlling rival hypotheses, using multiple complementary methods, and partnering with local collaborators. Dedicating attention to these ethical and cultural considerations results in greater confidence in policy recommendations.

Discussion

An intelligence analyst noted that when work has to be completed within 24 hours, an analyst might not have time to reflect on herself or the scenario from an ethical perspective. She wondered how to make space for these important considerations when in "go-mode." An intelligence analyst highlighted the ethical decision of whether to use certain data to answer a question while in "go-mode"—one that might require telling the policy maker that the answer is unknowable (e.g., it is unethical to justify a policy recommendation based on the results of a push poll), even if that contradicts the culture of the IC and its incentives. Bond suggested developing strategies to think through these issues *before* a high-pressure situation arises—for example, by creating an ethical code that guides every step of the work whether or not in crisis mode. She emphasized that analysts and researchers alike should always be in "ethical go-mode," continually protecting themselves and others who are helping to complete the work. She encouraged a more concerted effort to create this detailed guidance ahead of time to avoid having to make judgment calls during high-pressure situations that could incite mistakes, because anyone using data from humans about humans is responsible for their care and the care of the people who provided those data. Mampilly remarked that the *Analytic Framework* provides an ethics checklist as a starting point for any research that is being evaluated to make policy recommendations. He also urged the IC to foster a "culture of ethics." He described the immense pressure on junior analysts who want to make both actionable and ethical recommendations—ethics should not be compromised to make actionable recommendations, but a culture shift is required to embrace this mindset. An intelligence analyst explained that experienced intelligence analysts who have completed graduate studies have been introduced to these ethical standards, but new analysts have not had the opportunity to think deeply about ethical considerations and would benefit from additional guidance.

Pasek proposed removing the sole ethical *responsibility* from the person who is making the decision (similar to the use of research ethics boards in biomedical and behavioral science) so that the motivation for analysis does not overshadow the ethics of the analysis (i.e., give someone else the power to put an "ethics stop" on the work). In this case, however, ethics would still be *considered* by everyone involved in the process, as it should be in any investigation that includes human subjects. Bond pointed out the danger in asking people to separate themselves from their responsibility for ethical decisions. She reiterated that every analyst who engages with data from humans about humans has an individual responsibility, equivalent to that of anyone else in the hierarchy; in other words, ethical responsibility extends beyond ethical practice in data collection to ethical use of the data. James Druckman (expert contributor for the *Analytic Framework* and Payson S. Wild Professor of Political Science at Northwestern University) supported Pasek's commentary about relying on external entities to make ethical judgments but suggested first considering the motivations of external sources. Thus, while it might be difficult to trust oneself, it could be equally difficult to identify an entity that could be wholly trusted to provide ethical guidance. Bautista referenced the American Statistical Association's code of ethics, which highlights a practitioner's responsibilities to science, the public, research subjects, and colleagues. Such an ethical code is then internalized in the work and reflected in the work products. An analyst indicated that implementers also play an important role in the ethical conduct of research. Because some are willing to do dangerous research for profit or because of ideology, he advised caution on behalf of those implementers.

Addressing Mampilly's earlier discussions about different administrations' influences on collaboration between academia and the IC, Faranda proposed that this relationship be normalized. When an administration changes, the IC continues to do its best analysis; however, during times of political tension, support from the academic community is even more critical. Mampilly agreed that the IC is not as politicized as the broader society and can work objectively across administrations; however, academics do not always share that mindset. He suggested dedicating time to creating a healthier relationship between the two communities. Michael Hout (expert contributor for the *Analytic Framework* and professor of sociology at New York University) observed a difference between career employees and political appointees. For example, even when career employees experience political pressure to change how they do their jobs, most do not, perhaps owing to the support of academia and organizations like the National Academies and the Population Association of America. Diana Mutz (expert contributor for the *Analytic Framework*, and Samuel A. Stouffer Chair in Political Science and Communication and director of the Institute for the Study of Citizens and Politics at the University of Pennsylvania) added that academics who have interacted with the National Science Foundation through various administrations have been told that their cooperation with the IC is valuable. However, she said that it is important for the IC to communicate more broadly its desire to work closely with academia because those external to the government might be unaware.

Faranda reflected on the current situation in Ukraine, where analysts have asked whether it is ethical to conduct survey research. Her office uses the AAPOR code as a guide, which prioritizes "do no harm." Important questions to consider include the following: are people being put at risk or being retraumatized? Or, are people being given an opportunity to have their voices heard? She underscored that a checklist of potential harms could serve as an initial guide for decision making. D. Sunshine Hillygus (expert contributor for the *Analytic Framework,* and professor of political science and professor of public policy [by courtesy] at Duke University) commented that ethics and the potential harm of research are difficult to conceptualize in the abstract. Some researchers are unaware of the type of harm that survey research can cause—for example, via associated disclosure risk. While that might not be an issue if data are not made publicly available, other issues arise when data are collected without explicit consent or are used in ethically unsound ways. Although the AAPOR checklist is suitable to assess transparency and quality, she posited that it could have limited use to assess ethical issues. She wondered how best to think about the questions researchers could be asking; for example, her checklist as a university institutional review board member is likely less comprehensive than what would be useful for an intelligence analyst. Bond explained that an analyst can ask herself certain questions to target higher-level ethical concerns: Were the data provided voluntarily? Where are the respondents located in terms of their power to protect themselves? Where is the survey conductor located? For example, even with a phone survey, a phone line could be re-identified and people could listen in, which could cause harm to individuals. It is critical to think about these issues ahead of time and evaluate their context within broader cultural concerns. She cautioned that relying only on an ethics "checklist" is insufficient, as ethical considerations are far more complicated.

Gelfand said that these issues relate to "ethical climate," not "individual ethical style," and a change would need to be implemented over the long term. She advocated for the development of a set of practices and rewards to improve the "ethical climate" and to make ethics a top priority in the IC. She emphasized that this shift requires both training and thought experiments with feedback as well as local collaboration to help intelligence analysts make the most ethical decisions.

2

Hypothetical Applications of the *Analytic Framework*

Charles Lau (co-lead expert contributor for the *Analytic Framework* and director of the International Survey Research Program at RTI International) invited expert contributors, paper authors, and members of the intelligence community (IC) to consider the following four hypothetical scenarios that an intelligence analyst might encounter as an exercise in applying the guidance from the foundational layer of the *Analytic Framework* (NASEM, 2022).

SCENARIO 1: EVALUATION OF POLITICAL SUPPORT IN A MULTI-ETHNIC COUNTRY

Lau provided an overview of the first scenario, which was developed by the workshop planning committee and is presented in Table 2-1.

Evaluation of Data Sources

Elizabeth Zechmeister (co-lead expert contributor for the *Analytic Framework*, and Cornelius Vanderbilt Professor of Political Science and director of the Latin American Public Opinion Project at Vanderbilt University) observed that because the research question was assigned to the analyst and data are available, the first step is to narrow the scope, with consideration for the quality and potential use of the data. To evaluate the credibility and soundness of each of the three datasets, she suggested that Rachel consult the first paper in the foundational layer of the *Analytic Framework*, "Drawing Inferences from Public Opinion Surveys: Insights

TABLE 2-1 Scenario 1

Scenario	Description
IC analyst	Rachel is an early career IC analyst with limited background in survey research.
Country	Multi-ethnic, low-income country.
IC analyst task	Rachel is tasked with summarizing the public's attitudes about the prime minister within 5 business days, with a focus on variation by ethnic groups.
Data sources available	Rachel has access to the following: (1) a high-quality face-to-face survey conducted by the U.S. Department of State 2 years ago; (2) a well-executed mobile phone survey conducted by the U.S. Department of State 3 months ago; and (3) an online poll from last week conducted by the dominant political party and published on the party's website, with minimal documentation. Individual-level (micro) data are available for (1) and (2) but not (3).

for Intelligence Reports," by René Bautista (associate director of the Methodology and Quantitative Social Sciences department at NORC, University of Chicago).

Online Poll

Zechmeister posited that Rachel's first inclination might be to eliminate the online poll owing to its low credibility (i.e., it is not conducted by an objective organization, the goal of study could likely have been to present a positive attitude toward the dominant political party, and no documentation exists of the data collection process or who conducted the poll) and low soundness (i.e., the sampling approach is nonprobability with limited coverage of those with low socioeconomic status, offering only a glimpse into the opinions of a fraction of the population of interest). Using Bautista's rating system, Rachel would likely categorize the poll as "not credible, not sound" and notice that it is impossible to disaggregate the data to assess variation across ethnic groups.

William "Chip" Eveland (expert contributor for the *Analytic Framework*, and professor of communication and professor of political science [by courtesy] at The Ohio State University) noted that, depending on the nature of the country and the extent to which the results of the poll drift from the dominant party's Website into public understanding, *representations* of public opinion often influence public opinion. While the online poll has many disadvantages and might not reliably portray actual public opinion, it could still have value in showing Rachel what the population *perceives* as public opinion, which could shape future public opinion.

Scott Page (expert contributor for the *Analytic Framework* and John Seely Brown Distinguished University Professor of Complexity, Social Science, and Management at the University of Michigan) suggested that Rachel visit the Website and attempt to determine who ran the poll to see whether they had also run previous polls. As noted in the discussion of poll averaging in the *Analytic Framework*, a time series of bad polls can reveal a lot of information; even if the mean is wrong, the direction might be meaningful (NASEM, 2022).

He also noted that this poll will have both sampling and nonsampling errors; nevertheless, Rachel might still estimate the upper bound of the prime minister's support, which could prove useful. He also advised that Rachel consider how proportions of ethnic groups have changed in the past 2 years. If they have been stable, the face-to-face survey conducted by the U.S. Department of State 2 years prior could be valuable; if the proportions have changed, the online poll could be beneficial in revealing a worst- or best-case scenario for the prime minister.

Zechmeister summarized that although the dataset is ranked low on both credibility and soundness, Rachel should not immediately dismiss it because it illuminates the information environment surrounding the population. Page remarked that in some cases, perception is reality. For example, in 2017 Delphi Analytica claimed that Kid Rock had more support for a Senate seat than the sitting senator Debbie Stabenow, an assertion that was widely spread through the media and took Stabenow's team much time to counteract. Thus, it is important for Rachel to know that she could test quickly to determine whether the poll is gaining traction in the social media sphere and whether the perception matters.

Face-to-Face Survey

Eveland posited that to evaluate the data from the face-to-face survey, Rachel would consult "Drawing Inferences from Public Opinion Surveys: Insights for Intelligence Reports" as well as "Ascertaining True Attitudes in Survey Research," by Kanisha Bond (assistant professor of political science at Binghamton University, State University of New York). The survey is of good quality, and face-to-face is a "gold standard" for representation, especially in a low-income country. The credibility of these data seems high, but the soundness could be questionable given the assigned task. He suggested that Rachel think carefully about three issues when evaluating the usefulness of this dataset:

1. Considering that the goal is to describe public attitudes toward the prime minister and how they vary by a country's ethnic groups, and

sample size is the central determinant of margin of error, which ethic subgroup can be described with what degree of accuracy?
2. Owing to the nature of the interviews, the interviewer effects could be amplified, especially when the ethnicities of the interviewer and interviewee are mismatched. Would consulting the available micro-level data, with the assistance of a colleague with more experience, help reveal any biases?
3. Since the data were collected 2 years ago, is public opinion stable?

Zechmeister added that Rachel could look at the documentation accompanying the data to understand how the questions were asked as well as the political climate (e.g., how openly people could express their opinions). This face-to-face survey could also provide a point of comparison for the approval rating with newer datasets.

Page explained that because the relative size of the ethnic groups is known and data on how much they support the prime minister are available, Rachel could calculate what the expected vote total should have been—resulting in a "budget balance" between support and electoral results. If Rachel has access to the questions asked, Page continued, she should ensure that the survey questions were not phrased to meet preconceived objectives. Perhaps more important, since Rachel is a novice, he suggested that she write down what she thinks the data will reveal *before* looking at them to prevent being biased; if the results do not align with her hypotheses, it might be worthwhile for her to consult with a senior analyst to understand whether the flaw is in the hypothesis or the data.

Mobile Phone Survey

Page commented that if the mobile phone survey is divided by ethnic group, it is likely both credible and sound; however, considering the commentary on survey language selection from Michele Gelfand (expert contributor for the *Analytic Framework;* John H. Scully Professor in Cross-Cultural Management and professor of organizational behavior, Stanford Graduate School of Business; and professor of psychology [by courtesy], School of Humanities and Sciences, Stanford University), a question arises about how to account for nonresponse that could have been caused by a language barrier. These cultural considerations could be intensified in the mobile phone survey.

Emphasizing the value of comparing datasets to deepen understanding, Page directed Rachel to review the *Analytic Framework's* "Integrating Data Across Sources," by Josh Pasek (associate professor of communication and media and political science, faculty associate in the Center for Political Studies, and core faculty for the Michigan Institute for Data Science at the

University of Michigan) and Sunghee Lee (research associate professor at the Institute for Social Research at the University of Michigan). It is also important for Rachel to consider any events of the past 3 months that could indicate that the mobile phone survey data are outdated, although Page noted that the mobile phone survey is still likely more useful than the face-to-face survey given its comparative timeliness.

Referencing both "Drawing Inferences from Public Opinion Surveys: Insights for Intelligence Reports" and "Ascertaining True Attitudes in Survey Research," Eveland pointed out that mobile phone surveys allow people to avoid answering certain questions more easily than face-to-face surveys. He encouraged Rachel to pay close attention to the "do not know" or "refuse" answers in both the face-to-face and mobile phone surveys as a point of comparison to understand whether the survey mode influenced the results. However, he agreed with Page that the mobile phone survey is still likely to be more useful than the face-to-face survey given that it was conducted more recently.

Zechmeister anticipated that Rachel would spend the most time assessing this dataset, especially to gauge its soundness in relation to her specific goal. She also urged Rachel to think about the sample and mode effects. For example, was this a high-quality random-digit-dial survey, which is uncommon in this context, or did the survey firm draw from a list, which is more common, and what was the coverage? Zechmeister's research indicates that samples can skew toward higher socioeconomic status groups with phone-based approaches; therefore, Rachel would consider whether the survey contains sufficient information on the sample and the available weights. "Drawing Inferences from Public Opinion Surveys: Insights for Intelligence Reports" provides evidence that suggests that people might be more honest over the phone than in-person. Zechmeister asserted that this might not hold when the person lives in an autocratic country that is believed to tap phones. In that case, the mobile phone survey could be more biased than the face-to-face survey owing to self-censoring. Page added that local uprisings should also be a point of concern—ongoing research explores the extent to which mobile phones make uprisings easier owing to increased connectivity. However, in some countries, 20–40 percent of the people do not have mobile phones, so the socioeconomic status bias within an ethnic group could be high.

Discussion

A representative from the IC pointed out that because she would not have time to analyze the sources as deeply within the 5-day window, prioritization would be necessary. She thought that the 2-year-old survey was outdated, especially since the question at hand relates to attitudes toward a politician, and noted that she would most likely focus on the mobile phone survey. One strategy could be to review previous mobile phone surveys and compare them to face-to-face surveys conducted at the same time to determine whether historic response differences between the modes exist. Knowing whether the prime minister has made policy changes in the past 2 years that could be relevant for the ethnic groups of interest would also be useful; if not, the ethnic breakdown from the face-to-face survey could be used to better understand trends in attitudes. She asked the expert contributors about best practices to recognize interviewer effects, especially with only 5 days to conduct the analysis. Eveland replied that the microlevel data available for the face-to-face and mobile phone surveys could be used to gauge the presence of interviewer effect. He said that when a random code is assigned to each interviewer and characteristics such as gender and ethnic group are documented, it is possible to understand whether interviewers of the same ethnic group as the respondents received a different average response than the interviewers who are of a different ethnic group than the respondents.

The analyst inquired about comparing the achieved demographics in all three datasets with the known demographics of the country. Zechmeister described that as an essential first step and noted that information from census data could help to understand representation. Page pointed out that the group of interest is the proportion of the ethnic group over age 18 (i.e., voters). Ashley Amaya (senior survey methodologist at Pew Research Center) remarked that depending on the size of each ethnic group in the sample, the variance can change as can the stability of the estimates being created. The size would also affect Rachel's ability to do interviewer analysis. It is important to understand the way in which the sample was drawn (e.g., random sample versus cluster design), something for which an early career analyst like Rachel might not be prepared. Pasek observed that the face-to-face and mobile phone surveys might be very different in the context of varied ethnic groups. For example, if the mobile phone survey is done well and mobile phone coverage is good, a clear picture of the ethnic groups could emerge. He suggested that Rachel compare the weighted face-to-face survey with the unweighted mobile phone survey to confirm that all populations were appropriately covered and thereby determine whether the design achieved its goals. Page mentioned that not everyone within a particular ethnic group has a mobile phone, which could lead to a nonrepresentative sample. Members of an ethnic group could also reside in multiple locations, only some of which might support mobile phone use. Therefore, it could be useful for Rachel to separate urban and rural, north and south, and east and west to better understand the potential for an uprising—the interaction between region and ethnic group is key in this analysis. Building on Amaya's and Pasek's comments, Eveland highlighted the value of having access to detailed, technical information about how the face-to-face and mobile phone surveys were conducted. Courtney Kennedy (expert contributor for the *Analytic Framework* and director of survey research at Pew Research Center) noted that it is expensive to interview in multiple languages and usually not all of the languages will be covered. Thus, it would be valuable for Rachel to analyze the language distribution for each subgroup of interest and determine how well the survey covered those languages.

The analyst wondered how to determine the shelf-life of the face-to-face survey. Eveland suggested using a country-specific estimate of over-time variability. Pasek advocated for analysis within subgroups in the face-to-face survey and the mobile phone survey: even if the mobile phone data are lacking entire populations, if the populations that are well represented in both surveys have similar estimates, they could be used as a basis for asserting relative similarity. Page added that because some parties have ethnic affiliations, it is important for Rachel first to determine whether the prime minister is from a party that has historic ethnic affiliations.

The analyst posed a question about how polls of performance compare to polls of favorability. Eveland responded with an example from U.S. history: Bill Clinton's personal favorability plummeted during his presidency although his performance rating remained high. Such a situation would be challenging to evaluate across different datasets. Zechmeister said that Rachel could use other questions in the database to understand opinions of the prime minister with respect to either performance rating or favorability.

Another intelligence analyst asked what resources could be used to assess bias in the datasets if the face-to-face survey was not available as a point of comparison. Bautista observed that the producer of the face-to-face and mobile phone surveys is a "reliable data producer," owing to its connection to the U.S. Department of State. This producer likely has other work that could be consulted, which would include more systematic indicators that could provide a better sense of the modes and changes within them. Pasek suggested that Rachel first think about the mobile phone coverage, broadband access, and linguistic distribution in the country. The next step is to determine whether anything else that is happening in the country might be of interest, in that it could have introduced differences between surveys that might be significant. Comparing datasets on attributes that should not have changed can be an important indicator of confidence in the data and increase the likelihood that differences between the datasets are indicative of substantive changes. Page wondered about possible error—for example, whether the survey being relied upon incorrectly suggests that something significant has happened, or the survey incorrectly suggests that nothing has happened. Amaya pointed out that even people with extensive statistics experience deliberate when to use weights and which weights to use—an issue that could be discussed, in this case, with Rachel's supervisor. It is also important to account for complex samples when analyzing the data, which affect variance estimation—a feature on which only an expert in survey research would be focused. Another analyst commented that all of these types of questions will arise again in the future; this accumulating knowledge will be useful the next time an early career analyst like Rachel finds herself in "go-mode."

SCENARIO 2: REACTION TO A MILITARY COUP

Kennedy provided an overview of the second scenario, which was developed by the workshop planning committee and is presented in Table 2-2.

Approaches to the Research Question and the Data Collection

Kennedy remarked that a coup presents particular challenges, especially in terms of posing a research question. Lisa Mueller (expert contributor for the *Analytic Framework* and associate professor of political science at Macalester College) explained that in the aftermath of a coup, Tanya would likely be most interested in the stability of the society. For example, will there be a counter-coup? If that research question is selected, the population of interest would be the members of the military. Another important question could relate to the safety of the society; for example, will there be a popular uprising in response to the coup? If this research question is chosen, the population of interest would include members of the society as a whole rather than the military. It is also important for Tanya to monitor lines of communication among members of the new government and the citizens. For instance, did the government promise to hold free and fair elections within a specific time period, and has it followed through? Has public opinion changed? What information do the government and the citizens have about each other?

TABLE 2-2 Scenario 2

Scenario	Description
IC analyst	Tanya is a mid-level analyst with 5 years of experience working with surveys.
Country	Middle-income country. This country is an important security partner of the United States in a strategic region. The country recently experienced a military coup, and there are significant security challenges in the northern part of the country. The government has declared a state of emergency, so face-to-face surveys are not feasible.
IC analyst task	Tanya is tasked with developing a plan for how the State Department can understand public opinion within 1 month.
Data sources available	Tanya has access to no existing data sources.

Mueller emphasized that an intelligence analyst's inferences about the military and the broader society are only part of the task; inferences about what these groups know about each other would also be useful.

D. Sunshine Hillygus (expert contributor for the *Analytic Framework*, and professor of political science and professor of public policy [by courtesy] at Duke University) agreed that Tanya should first identify which measures of public opinion are most important: is the goal of the research to evaluate the coup, the overthrown government, or the United States? Tanya would then want to determine what kinds of new data collection are possible given the time frame and the feasibility of reaching individuals, since face-to-face surveys are not an option in this scenario.

Mueller added that Tanya might also be interested in understanding how people view the new leader after the coup has concluded. Because this new leader has gained power through force, he or she likely will rely more heavily on charisma to remain in office than an elected official would, and people might use unreliable cues to make decisions about the leader's competence (e.g., physical attractiveness). Mueller indicated that both the members of the society and the intelligence analyst are in a low-information environment in this scenario; therefore, it is important for Tanya to determine what information people in the society actually have. The question guiding the research might then be the following: what do people think of the new leader based on the limited information they have after the coup? Hillygus suspected that measurement problems could arise with this question because people might be afraid or unwilling to share their real opinions—surveys might not provide valuable information for this reason. Instead, Tanya's next step could be to scrape social media data to understand the extent of existing biases in the population.

Reflecting on other possible strategies to gather new data, Kennedy explained that if Tanya decides to conduct a survey, a phone poll or online data collection might be the best approaches. If phone services are still available after the coup, a phone poll could provide good representation. However, as Hillygus observed, the measurement properties might be flawed, especially if the coup was violent. If online data collection is deemed the more appropriate approach, Kennedy suggested that Tanya focus on a nonprobability, convenience-type collection. Although a self-administered online survey would increase the likelihood of honest responses, the representation would not be as strong as that of a phone poll. Hillygus highlighted the emergence of subpopulations that might be of interest in providing benchmarks even if their opinions do not represent the population as a whole.

Discussion

A representative from the IC inquired about how a survey question in this scenario could be phrased in a safe way to encourage truthful responses. Kennedy proposed focusing on respondents' levels of optimism for the future of their country as one approach. Keeping practical measurement instruments in mind, Mueller pointed out that this is a middle-income country, likely with reliable access to the Internet. Therefore, Internet polling might be the preferred approach—and one that offers advantages over Short Message Service (SMS)- or voice-based polls because it could employ an endorsement or list experiment. Mueller acknowledged that although these types of experiments have drawbacks, they could help Tanya to understand aggregate attitudes toward the new leadership. Bond suggested that Tanya try to understand implicit attitudes by probing the emotional underpinnings of those attitudes with the following types of survey questions: How do you feel right now? Are you afraid? Are you hopeful? Are you confused? What is your primary concern at the moment? She added that it would be useful for Tanya to compare responses by location within the country to gain context and to better understand any connections between the stability in attitudes and physical circumstances. Hillygus supported this focus on implicit direct measures of mass attitudes as well as the value of understanding geographic variation in these attitudes. She described several tradeoffs for Tanya to consider when thinking about the allocation of research resources: high response rate, maximum coverage, or deep opinions. She cautioned against posing open-ended research questions given the time frame allotted for this task and suggested that Tanya prioritize the understanding of geographic differences.

Zechmeister posed a question about how to evaluate the validity of responses to online surveys. Hillygus replied that people's willingness to tell the truth is the most pressing issue with an online survey. If a survey infrastructure already exists in the country of interest, including panels of people familiar with answering online survey questions, a separate set of concerns arises about the likelihood of fraudulent responses in order to receive incentives. Hillygus advocated that a measure allowing for a data quality check (e.g., paradata on start and end times) be included in all surveys.

An analyst asked how to assess whether the results of an experiment are reliable in an environment where no previous data are available for comparison. Mueller explained that in a list experiment, for example, people would not be asked direct questions about their attitudes toward the new government. Instead, several attitudes (~5) would be included in a list, including a "sensitive" attitude, and participants would be asked which apply to them. Not all of the participants receive the same list; usually only half receive a list that includes the sensitive item. She asserted that the success of this approach does not rely on the availability of previous high-quality data; rather, it relies on the quality of the design of the experiment. The value of experimental data is related more to how well an experiment is designed—ensuring randomization and prioritizing sample size—than to how it is executed. She emphasized that, in this scenario, a list experiment could be rolled out within a few weeks of the coup. Hillygus responded that if SMS is selected as the best method for data collection, a list experiment could be too difficult to implement. Early in the planning stage, she continued, Tanya could seek existing data (e.g., a census) to determine benchmarks, as it is unrealistic that no previous data are available. Tanya could then consider the infrastructure that could constrain new data collection and narrow the scope of what would be feasible. Kennedy added that a list experiment might be worth testing; however, she cautioned that although list experiments seem excellent in theory, they often do not perform as well in practice (i.e., list experiment data do not always make sense). She reiterated Mueller's assertion that list experiments have to be designed flawlessly to be successful. Hillygus shared Kennedy's concerns about list experiments and noted that interpretability (especially with automated or SMS surveys) as well as the level of confidence Tanya would have in the results could be problematic, especially if no previous data are available. Pasek underscored that it is possible to test the validity of list experiments by correlating their microdata with other measures. Mueller emphasized that every method is susceptible to imperfect design and/or implementation. She expressed her support for endorsement and list experiments because they are relatively low cost and well suited for the context of this scenario; it could also be valuable for Tanya to triangulate the evidence from such experiments with other evidence.

Hillygus agreed that all methods have both advantages and disadvantages, and Tanya should weigh those in the planning stages. In a context where no previous survey data exist, it is important to evaluate social media environments and their data as well as how value could be extracted from those data. Even though no data source is perfect, she continued, Tanya should still ensure that the methods she selects will extract worthwhile information. She encouraged Tanya to consider the sources of administrative data, the reach of social media, and any analysis that could be performed on those data to understand changes that occurred in the population pre- and post-coup. Amaya added that social media data could be useful in this scenario *if* the platforms are still active. She agreed with Hillygus that change in attitude over time is an important feature that could be gathered from an analysis of social media data—and people on social media might be those most likely to react to the coup. Such an analysis should focus not only on the text but also on the emoticons and links, she continued, which requires training and computer power that Tanya might not have. Bautista commented that a middle-income country would be home to researchers who have collected data in the region using innovative approaches; thus, Tanya could identify these researchers in the northern part of the country and gather their insights.

Another analyst remarked that a situation in which no previous data exist is highly uncommon, and he suggested that Tanya ask local implementers for assistance in identifying data sources. Even with well-developed dictionaries, he cautioned Tanya against drawing samples from social media data in this particular scenario, as many of the platforms are more niche in middle-income countries than in the United States. If previous relationships with research firms exist in this country, Tanya could invite panels back from a previous probability-based face-to-face survey, if it could be done safely. He also advised Tanya to avoid conducting a list experiment over the phone in this scenario, owing in part to its substantial cognitive burden. Although it might be difficult to measure attitudes directly (e.g., it would be unethical to ask questions that could trigger trauma for or endanger respondents), he emphasized the value of understanding how people are feeling in this scenario. To begin to understand these feelings, it would be useful for Tanya to know whether the country is democratic and if it recently held elections. Furthermore, because coups are not usually a surprise, studying relevant pre-coup conversation could help Tanya to make inferences about people's current feelings.

An analyst asked the experts to elaborate on the concept of rolling data collection. Lau explained that for SMS approaches with random-digit dialing, people receive text message surveys with 10–15 questions each. This method is best suited for brief, simple survey questions. However, he has observed significant heterogeneity in the quality of panels and the information they provide to produce high-quality data. For example, some panels are probability based, drawn from regularly updated mobile network operator databases, are high quality and accurate, and provide good coverage. The auxiliary data from the frame are suitable for nonresponse adjustments, for example, because response rates to SMS-based surveys are typically low and these types of panels have often skewed more male, urban, and educated. Other panels are more suspicious, with different standards for quality, and are often targeted for market research. Lau encouraged analysts to ask many questions of a panel provider: how was the sample drawn? What is the coverage? Are data from the frame available? He directed analysts to the American Association for Public Opinion Research's (AAPOR's) Transparency Initiative,[1] which includes guidance on expectations for providers. Even when biases arise with these

---

[1] For information about this initiative, see https://www.aapor.org/transparency_initiative.htm.

SMS surveys, having data over time can illustrate trends—that is, even if the data are not particularly valid, they can be useful when combined with other sources of data. Pasek cautioned about ensuring that the samples under comparison are consistent, particularly with the more marketing-oriented firms.

Contemplating other design options, Hillygus suggested that Tanya conduct a recontact study of an existing probability survey, using SMS (which is low burden and can reveal geographic movement) to increase responses from those in the northern part of the country. She also proposed the use of refreshment samples (i.e., a fresh panel recruit), which provide the opportunity to assess attrition or other types of panel effects. Kennedy agreed with Hillygus that a recontact study of a pre-coup probability panel could be the best option, and a new phone or SMS survey could also be conducted. A less established, opt-in panel might be possible, depending on the country and the vendor. She also cautioned that much of the literature on data quality from opt-in online panels is U.S.-centric, creating many knowledge gaps related to the international space. To try to circumvent positivity bias in nonprobability panels, she encouraged analysts to avoid posing yes/no and agree/disagree questions; instead, an ordinal scale or forced choice option would be more effective in this type of scenario.

Gelfand observed that because the experts are approaching this scenario from different disciplines, they approach problems in unique ways and use different language to refer to similar concepts. She discussed non-Western-based dictionary development to assess cultural constructs (see, e.g., Choi et al., 2022; Gelfand et al., 2015), which can help overcome any language differences and enhance the research process.

An analyst said that it might not be worthwhile for Tanya to try to implement anything within 1 month—if the coup has not ended, opinions might not be stable and the U.S. government does not have unlimited resources to field multiple data collection efforts. He expressed disbelief that Tanya would not have access to any historical data. He suggested that Tanya use the month to track those data down, study them, and consult with experts who are located in the United States and could provide insight to develop a plan for understanding public opinion in the country of interest. Although this scenario's discussion introduced several best practices for data collection, he continued, it did not consider the constraints for what analysts have to produce afterward. Analysts have to communicate to a generalist audience that might not be familiar with or convinced by new techniques; because it is not feasible to introduce advanced techniques to policy makers during a time of crisis, these conversations are most effective during times of peace.

SCENARIO 3: ANTICIPATION OF POLITICAL INSTABILITY

James Druckman (expert contributor for the *Analytic Framework* and Payson S. Wild Professor of Political Science at Northwestern University) provided an overview of the third scenario, which was developed by the workshop planning committee and is presented in Table 2-3.

Ethical Considerations

Druckman advised Luis to begin his analysis by dividing the surveys by country to determine which countries have more than one survey. Luis would then begin conducting an "ethics check" of each survey, with consideration both for moral issues and for potential long-term consequences related to the use of certain data. First, it is critical to ensure that the human research subjects were treated appropriately—protection from danger, verification of confidentiality, and confirmation of consent. This part of the ethical evaluation requires an understanding of the cultural context (e.g., inaccurate language translations would affect the understanding of consent) and a recognition that using unethical surveys could undermine future research efforts in the region.

Second, Druckman continued, it is important for Luis to verify that the data themselves are ethically sound. Guidelines from AAPOR, for example, would be especially useful in evaluating the ethics of data from an unstable region. Based on the information that accompanies the data, Luis could determine whether these data are appropriate for inference by ensuring transparency in how the data were collected, who paid for the data, who collected the data, how the data were analyzed, and where the data can be found.

TABLE 2-3 Scenario 3

Scenario	Description
IC analyst	Luis is an early career IC analyst with no background in survey research.
Region	Politically unstable *region* (~15 countries) with significant security challenges.
IC analyst task	Luis is tasked with describing public opinion in the region, with a focus on recommending countries where popular discontent with the regime might emerge in the next year.
Data sources available	20 surveys (5 mobile phone, 5 social media nonprobability Web surveys, 10 face-to-face) from the past 5 years. The surveys vary in quality: some follow highest quality standards (microdata available), some are low-cost/lower-quality surveys (microdata available), and some are poor quality (no microdata available).

Druckman explained that it is particularly important to understand how the sample was generated and how many people participated in the survey. For example, is information provided about the mobile phone coverage in a particular country? Are response rates for the mobile phone surveys provided? Is social media censored in a way that only some people would have access to a social media survey? Druckman cautioned that a lack of information about sample generation could lead Luis to use a problematic sample (e.g., the unethical use of data for something other than their intended purpose) and thus make a poor inference. Additional key ethical questions for Luis to consider include the following: does each survey include the date that it was given, and were the data collected recently enough to be worthwhile? Does each survey provide information about what measures were included? What techniques were used? Was there anonymity for participants? Was normalization performed? If all of the surveys are deemed unethical, Druckman indicated that Luis should look for new data; if some (or all) of the surveys are deemed ethical, their quality should be evaluated before making any inferences.

Quality Considerations

Lau discussed the "quality checks" that should be performed with each survey that has passed the ethics check. If these quality checks fail, an intelligence analyst would either have to collect new data or correct for the known errors; given that Luis is likely constrained by time in this scenario, Lau suggested that he focus on the latter.

Lau pointed out that Luis should have several concerns about the quality of the social media nonprobability Web surveys. Using the *Analytic Framework*, especially Bautista's Rating Tool for Survey Quality (see Figure 2-1), Luis would note that the stated purpose of the surveys might be different from the real purpose, and although the surveys are authentic, they might not be of high quality. It is clear who paid for the study, but because a few of the sponsors are political parties, the motivation for conducting the research is suspicious. Furthermore, the survey research team is unknown, the surveys have sampling and coverage problems, and the response rates are likely low. Given that these surveys have both low credibility and soundness, Luis would question whether these sources could be used. However, because these Web surveys could represent an upper bound of support for a particular leader, Lau urged Luis to consult with colleagues as well as to contemplate under what conditions he could use these Web surveys—what levels of credibility or soundness have to be achieved to trust this source, especially since other data are available?

Lau explained that although the mobile phone surveys might be more credible than the social media surveys, a lack of documentation about weighting suggests that the mobile phone surveys might not be nationally

	Credibility of contextual information	
Is the survey purpose clear?	No, it is not clear at all the objective of the survey.	………	Yes, it is clear what the study aims to do.
Is the survey authentic (not fake)?	No. The survey is clearly a fake.	………	Yes. The survey is clearly authentic.
Does the survey avoid condemned practices?	No. The study did not avoid condemned practices to collect survey data.	………	Yes. It is obvious that the survey was collected using condemned practices.
Is it clear who paid for the study?	No. Totally unclear who paid for the study.	………	Yes. Source of financing is quite clear and publicly known.
Is the team a known group of researchers?	No. No idea who designed and implemented the survey.	………	Yes. Survey research team is known and easily contactable.
Is the reputation of the survey agency known?	No. No one seems to know anything about the survey organization.	………	Yes. They are well known, they have good reputation in general, and they publicly report results.
Is the description of how the study was conducted clear?	No. Survey methodology is completely unavailable.	………	Yes. Documentation and write-up of results is very clear.

FIGURE 2-1 A rating tool for survey quality.
SOURCE: NASEM (2022).

representative. If the coverage of mobile phones in the countries of interest is only 40 to 80 percent, this method cannot reach a significant portion of the target population—the part of the population that is most likely unhappy with the regime. Therefore, Luis would have to assign bias to these surveys.

Lau reiterated that the *Analytic Framework* is not meant to be directive but rather to spark discussion: how does such a rating system work on a day-to-day basis for intelligence analysts? What challenges emerge? How can the guidance of the *Analytic Framework* be bridged with the practices of analysts?

Prediction Challenges

Druckman noted that the next step is to make an inference from each survey that has passed the ethics and quality checks. Luis could begin with measurement considerations such as whether a direct question was asked and if it was normalized. Privacy is a key concern; for example, did respondents feel protected while answering questions via phone or social media, or did they feel surveilled? It is also important for Luis to assess changes over time, as all of these surveys were conducted 5 years ago; if conditions have changed significantly or are changing quickly, these sources might not be useful in making predictions about the future. Druckman recalled that even though Luis does not have much experience with survey research, he knows the country context and thus can determine whether the predictions resonate as he makes comparisons across countries (e.g., whether the low-quality surveys are leading to unexpected predictions).

Druckman explained that with multiple sources of data from one country, Luis could consider integration using some of the basic techniques discussed in "Integrating Data Across Sources" (e.g., comparing surveys with different sampling frames to determine whether distinct populations had different levels of discontent and how they complement one another). Pasek suggested that Luis examine the following for meaningful comparisons: what do the high-quality data reveal? Are the methods of collecting data across countries similar? Are the surveys in the same language? Do the measures have similar meaning across cultures? If discontent is a low-probability outcome, he continued, then the relative question would be more about the variability than the mean. Thus, Luis might consider which metric would be predictive of future discontent, how that metric could be modeled, and whether similar sets of data from other regions could be included in the model. At this point, Luis could determine whether and where the high-quality data match the low-quality data and begin making inferences about volatility. Pasek urged Luis to add measures early in this process that would enable the interpretation of the lower-quality data. For example, information about mobile phone and social media use collected during a face-to-face survey would be helpful for calibration when the lower-quality surveys emerge. He highlighted more sophisticated models that could be employed to reveal trends over time, which could be built with the 20 available data sources if the differences between them are calibrated well and microdata are available. He stressed that much of this depends on the eventual metric—the predictor of discontent—which is more likely to emerge between samples rather than in one sample.

Lau added that because this scenario raises questions about cross-cultural differences, measurement equivalence and cultural norms that influence response styles are key considerations. He contemplated how these considerations would influence the IC's practice, and he encouraged workshop participants to identify related gaps in the *Analytic Framework* and to discuss how they could be addressed.

Discussion

A representative from the IC observed that an early career intelligence analyst could be challenged and overwhelmed by an assignment to conduct regional analysis and would likely take several months to complete it. She encouraged Luis to consult with experts as well as to take advantage of the ethics and quality checklists in the *Analytic Framework*. In order for Luis to make any valid conclusions, it is important to note that even if the sources are reliable, much information will be missing from 20 surveys over 5 years and 15 countries. Before assessing the surveys country by country to perform the ethics and quality checks, she suggested that Luis list information available over time by country. Given the task's focus on discontent with the regime, it is also important to ensure that the survey respondents were able to speak freely and that the purpose of the study was transparent. The analyst posited that the checklists could make it possible for Luis to develop either low or high levels of confidence in the information from each country; additional conversation within the IC about developing confidence when information is limited or outdated could be beneficial. After determining the level of confidence and identifying key gaps, Luis could explore social or traditional media analysis, event data indicative of instability, or any other data related to consumer sentiment to better understand the level of discontent. Lastly, the analyst emphasized the cross-cultural component of this scenario; even though the question focuses on a region, she urged Luis first to look at the data country-by-country and then to reaggregate those data to a region. Page noted that although process can reduce human decision-making bias, it can breed overconfidence: despite having access to 20 surveys, Luis's prediction task in this scenario is very difficult. Page proposed that Luis take the union of the confidence intervals to reveal the level of uncertainty.

Another analyst said that she would be inclined to eliminate the social media nonprobability Web surveys in this scenario but wondered whether something useful could be gleaned from them. Druckman replied that it depends on what other sources are available; it would be difficult to eliminate any data that would pass a basic ethics test if limited data were available. He suggested thinking about the coverage, the nature of social media, and the sample that is gathered (in terms of different benchmarks) to determine whether the surveys have any value before eliminating them. Pasek added that a few recent social media data points might reveal significant information about the level of volatility in a region, which could aid in making a prediction about future discontent. Druckman commented that any measures that help to understand people's emotions toward the regime could reveal precursors to discontent. Amaya suggested searching social media for the number of new pages and groups that have emerged, as well as how their membership is increasing. Since Luis is tasked with making a prediction, she continued, those paradata might be more useful than the posts themselves. Bautista mentioned that if the social media posts are studied, they could be viewed as sources of qualitative data on a particular sentiment.

When comparing the mobile phone surveys to the face-to-face surveys, the analyst wondered how to determine what is closer to true attitude if a systematic difference in attitude emerges. Lau highlighted sample coverage as one key factor (i.e., mobile phone surveys exclude people without mobile phones) and suggested subsetting the face-to-face survey data to make a fair comparison. Another approach is to distinguish sampling and representation issues from measurement; for example, people might be more comfortable disclosing the truth on a sensitive issue over the phone than in person. Although that might suggest that the mobile phone surveys are producing the "truer" attitudes, that notion has to be balanced against issues of representation. In this instance, it would be worthwhile to consider which groups are systematically excluded from mobile phone surveys due to coverage and nonresponse and the extent to which these groups vary across the outcome being measured (e.g., discontent). Because this type of qualitative analysis relies on interpretation and inferences made by the analyst and communicated to the policy maker, Lau encouraged more discussion within the IC on this issue. Kennedy indicated that Luis could stack the mobile phone dataset and the face-to-face dataset to create one dataset and predict the attitude (the predictor variables would be the commonalities between the two datasets, such as demographics, and the variable for the mode). When controlling for the compositional differences between these two datasets (e.g., region, age, sex, and ethnic group), sometimes no mode effect exists because differences in the data stemmed from sample composition not mode effects. Pasek added that if one assumes that the differences are a result of a mean shift within an individual country, sophisticated models (e.g., Bayesian or Bayesian-adjacent) could be employed to help estimate the reasons for those differences. For example, he described a combination of generalized additive models, which generate a smooth plot over time, and multilevel models that account for differences between modes and between countries. Individual plots can be generated for each country assuming that the differences between the countries are relatively stable, with the exception of any added discontinuities—the effects of those discontinuities then become visible. Pasek mentioned that although an early career intelligence analyst like Luis would not be doing this type of work, the toolkit to do so exists.

Bautista stated that it would be helpful for Luis to understand the logic behind the measure. Reflecting on differences in modes, he explained that more "authentic" responses are typically gathered in the absence of an interviewer. However, it can be difficult to gauge how a data collection process occurred; for example, meanings are sometimes "negotiated" and questions discussed by both the interviewer and the respondent in a face-to-face survey, which is not possible in a Web survey. Understanding how the experience occurred helps to understand the limitations around the data. Bond championed the notion of thinking more deeply about the data collection process. For example, are there more opportunities to "skirt the question" in one mode over another? When aggregate trends are unexpected, she continued, it is worthwhile to think about the context in which the data were produced, which does not require any technical expertise.

Druckman underscored the difficulty of prediction, which requires an analyst to measure a latent *future* feeling. He encouraged Luis to think carefully about measurement in this scenario: what is the construct to be captured? Should discontent or something that precedes discontent be measured? He reiterated Page's warning about overconfidence in a given prediction, and Page added that relative rank ordering might be useful to achieve odds ratios and that a good prediction is a result of both strong survey methodology and strong theory underlying the survey. Lau pointed out that, in this scenario, the subgroups of the population that are most likely to have discontent that could lead to protest are of greatest interest. Therefore, a general population-based survey might not be the best approach to predict areas of future discontent, as is discussed in the *Analytic Framework's* "Alternatives to Probability-based Surveys Representative of the General Population for Measuring Attitudes," written by Amaya.

SCENARIO 4: REGIONAL PUBLIC REACTIONS TO A GEOPOLITICAL CRISIS AND SUSCEPTIBILITY TO FALSE NARRATIVES

Lau described the final scenario, which was generated by the workshop participants and is presented in Table 2-4.

This scenario was examined alongside a recent *Washington Post* article (Parker, 2022) on public opinion about the Russian invasion of Ukraine. The article references survey data from Gary Langer, a well-known U.S.-based researcher. A phone poll was conducted across Russia by "strong, independent survey research firms" 1 week into the invasion, over the course of 3 days, with 1,640 respondents. The poll asked whether respondents support the Russian "military operation" on Ukrainian territory, and the reported results were as follows: ~58 percent supported the action and ~23 percent opposed it, with ~6 percent undecided and a ~13 percent nonresponse rate. The article also references a Russian government-affiliated survey with a similar demographic breakdown but different results.

Evaluation of Data Credibility and Soundness

An analyst emphasized that because the respondents are living in dangerous conditions, an intelligence analyst should determine whether the poll questions were worded to elicit truthful responses. Zechmeister shared that because she was unable to download the data files that are linked in the *Washington Post* article, she would request them from the firm that conducted the poll and begin to assess credibility and soundness (with guidance from "Drawing Inferences from Public Opinion Surveys: Insights for Intelligence Reports") as well as address the analyst's inquiry

TABLE 2-4 Scenario 4

Scenario	Description
IC analyst	An experienced intelligence analyst.
Region	10 nations.
IC analyst task	The analyst is tasked with understanding the regional public reactions to a geopolitical crisis as well as the susceptibility to false narratives after a small, friendly, strategic partner is invaded by a nuclear power. The analyst is expected to present the first deliverable in 2 weeks, but the project will likely continue for 1 year.
Data sources available	~5 years of biannual mobile phone surveys in 5 of the 10 nations in the region and some yearly aggregate international polls, but no data exist for the remaining nations.

about whether the questions were worded to provoke strategic responses or censored responses (with guidance from "Ascertaining True Attitudes in Survey Research"). Zechmeister noted that this poll likely provides an upper-bound estimate, given that respondents might have been concerned about phone surveillance. Another analyst observed that a translator might be needed to conduct these assessments because the files contain the original questionnaire in Russian. Pasek mentioned that although most in the public opinion community know Langer's reputation well, if that was not the case, it would be important for the intelligence analyst to conduct research into his credibility.

An analyst wondered what information is available to the Russian public and media—the susceptibility to false narratives is particularly salient in this scenario—and explained that an intelligence analyst could benchmark questions in this poll against prior research conducted in the country to determine whether this poll is a credible data source. Eveland added that the *Washington Post* article offers value in terms of benchmarking against previous Russian invasions of neighboring countries. Pasek suggested evaluating specific subgroups within the data source based on previous knowledge of Russia, and another analyst asked how to handle the raw data and how additional information about subgroups could be useful. Pasek replied that an analyst could explore the following questions: do we expect differences in this context between age groups or between locations? If the belief is that public opinion was better in previous times of conflict, are the same types of groups who supported those conflicts supportive of the current conflict? He stressed that understanding whether these types of means align could help an analyst to determine the credibility of the current data source.

Analysts explained that policy makers are likely to read sources like this *Washington Post* article and would expect an intelligence analyst to have an opinion about its credibility immediately, without being given the time to wade through the accompanying documentation. Even if the instrument is partially biased, an analyst wondered whether the results of the poll would reveal demographic divisions that would be of interest. Another analyst noted that intelligence analysts would also have to be prepared to explain quickly and clearly to policy makers how the data from this *Washington Post* article interact with other available data and whether their overall assessment is affected.

Ethical Challenges

A representative from the IC wondered about the accuracy of the statistic provided in the *Washington Post* article that 23 percent of the Russian respondents "oppose the military operation." Given that criticizing the

Kremlin is a criminal offense, she expressed her surprise that this number is not lower. However, if the opposition toward this "military operation" is this high under such conditions, that could suggest that the actual percentage of opposition is even higher. Furthermore, she contemplated the ethics of asking people whether they support something if voicing opposition to it is illegal. Zechmeister noted that the percentage being reported as "approving of the military operation" (58 percent) might be an upper bound, and participants might be censoring their true attitudes. If phones are being tapped in this context, it is unethical for people to risk their safety to participate in a poll.

In her review of a translated version of the original questionnaire, Amaya observed that analyzing responses to the question "Do you think *the rest* of the country supports the military operation?" could have helped to better understand true attitudes (as opposed to analyzing the responses to the question that asked participants whether *they* support the "military operation"). Conducting a variety of analyses on the provided data points would help confirm whether the correlation is as high as presented in the *Washington Post* article. For example, instead of analyzing by age, the attitudes of people who spoke to friends or family in Ukraine in the past 2 weeks could have been compared to those of people who had not. Additionally, to gauge the effectiveness of Russian messaging, which might be a better indicator than the rates of approval for the "military operation," she said that responses to the question asking participants to identify the goals of the Russian military could have been analyzed.

Bautista referenced another document accompanying the poll data, which reported that 90 percent of the respondents were apprehensive about participating in the poll. An intelligence analyst's awareness of this type of context is essential to evaluate the quality of the data. An analyst observed that even if the phones are not being tapped in Russia, the perception that they could cause undue stress on poll respondents, which explains why 90 percent were apprehensive. He said that an analyst's expertise is key in a scenario like this one because, as Eveland and Pasek also mentioned, it would be useful to know whether Russia's 2008 or 2014 invasions (of Georgia and Crimea, respectively) provide context about the stability of public opinion—that is, how does the 58 percent approval rating cited in the *Washington Post* article compare to the approval ratings in those instances?

Following the guidance of the *Analytic Framework*, Eveland reiterated the importance of understanding the nature of the survey provider and how the public views that provider, which could also affect the results of the poll. Furthermore, it is important for the intelligence analyst to consider how opinion is shifting geographically—for example, people in urban areas might have greater access to uncensored media coverage and thus might be less likely to support the invasion. Reflecting on other potential data sources to gauge population sentiment or the surrounding information environment, Zechmeister wondered to what degree social media is accessible in Russia.

Kennedy acknowledged that much of the Russian public is provided with a specific narrative that is different from the truth, so people that claim to "support the military operation" might not realize what they are actually supporting. She wondered how the questionnaire and the measurement address those differences. Lau pointed out that the concept of "support" is ambiguous and interpretable among respondents, and Amaya suspected significant nonresponse biases in the poll results. Kennedy posited that additional opposition could be "hiding," perhaps in the nonresponses to the poll, and it would be helpful for an intelligence analyst to better understand the cooperation rate of the public. Bautista remarked that a journalist's perspective of survey results and how they should be reported would be different from that of a survey methodologist. For example, a disclaimer is included in the data files—but not reported in the article—about how the sensitivity of the questions should be taken into account in interpreting the results.

An analyst summarized the results of another survey conducted around the same time as that referenced in the *Washington Post* article, which had a higher approval rating but a similar opposition rating owing to the use of a different scale (i.e., the response options from which participants could choose were fewer). Kennedy commented that although the poll described in the *Washington Post* article seems to be credible, the measurement is arguably unethical, as participants are essentially being asked to self-report an active crime; thus, it would be difficult for the intelligence analyst to interpret or trust the data. She wondered if the published poll results could have a positive impact on global views of the Russian public since the opposition rating is higher than what is portrayed in the information environment. Pasek suggested taking a Bayesian approach to analyzing the poll results. For example, if previous assumptions were that the approval rating would be even higher than what is presented in the *Washington Post* article, he said that this should shift our views (because we assume that the observed value is a likely maximum). He also pondered the potential implications if the approval rating were lower than 50 percent. Amaya reiterated that while the phone poll might be useful, it includes a significant amount of measurement error, nonresponse bias, and ethical problems. She added that it would be beneficial for the analyst to study the reasons that respondents provided for "supporting the special military operation."

Discussion

Eveland asked whether "rally around the flag" is a common way to understand data. An analyst replied that "rally around the flag" is a common way to understand data. In the case of an attack within a particular country or a natural disaster, it relates to a temporary change in public opinion in response to the significant event that deviates from the normal narrative and recedes within weeks or months. Pasek remarked that while "rally around the flag" is useful in some cases, intelligence analysts likely rely on other phenomena to explain public opinion that do not appear in the academic literature. He wondered whether it would be helpful for academia and the IC to collaborate to discuss, describe, locate, and/or document those phenomena. An analyst supported Pasek's idea of collaborating to broaden the understanding and communication of other relevant theories. Another analyst agreed that it would be worthwhile to develop some of the phenomena that the IC recognizes that have not yet been articulated by academia. She added that when policy makers automatically assume "rally around the flag" as the justification for a particular public opinion, it is incumbent upon the IC to explain whether and how the phenomenon is more complicated. A third analyst observed that most stakeholders have enough knowledge to suggest "rally around the flag" as an explanation and to ask about margin of error; with this common vocabulary as a starting point, the IC can then refine the conversation with deeper analysis. Bautista asserted that additional guidance would be beneficial to understand the theories behind how the data were created (i.e., the survey science), not just how they were interpreted. The analyst added that talking to experts in the field is valuable because policy makers rely on the IC for advice; the *Analytic Framework* helps intelligence analysts to better understand the latest methodologies and thus better serve this policy-making community.

3

Lessons Learned and Future Pathways

INSIGHTS FROM THE *ANALYTIC FRAMEWORK*

Dylan Rebstock (program officer at the National Academies of Sciences, Engineering, and Medicine) invited workshop participants to share insights gleaned from their experiences with and discussions about the *Analytic Framework*.

Scott Page (expert contributor for the *Analytic Framework* and John Seely Brown Distinguished University Professor of Complexity, Social Science, and Management at the University of Michigan) said that although he does not work with surveys specifically, he thinks about the usefulness of different representations. He encouraged intelligence analysts to embrace the depth of the science, which includes a good statistical understanding of how to think about surveys; to understand the "art" of conducting surveys; and to emphasize the link between the survey and its purpose.

Courtney Kennedy (expert contributor for the *Analytic Framework* and director of survey research at Pew Research Center) reiterated that, if possible, intelligence analysts should carefully design approaches during periods of calm instead of waiting until "go-mode" to tackle difficult ethical issues and methodological challenges with new types of data. Page suggested that analysts ask themselves the following questions during those periods of calm: what is the set of questions that might be asked, and what is our cache of polling information? What information assets are available, how often are they needed, and how often are they rerun? Josh Pasek (associate professor of communication and media and political science, faculty associate in the Center for Political Studies, and core faculty for the

Michigan Institute for Data Science at the University of Michigan) agreed that analysts should lay the groundwork for the unexpected situations that could arise by developing a baseline of questions, which also makes it easier to recognize how old data relate to new data.

An intelligence analyst remarked that the depth of the workshop's conversation about ethics was unexpected. Even though ethically challenging situations always arise, analysts do not spend as much time discussing them. Reflecting on the final scenario discussed during the workshop, he questioned whether obtaining some measurement, even if it is flawed and ethical boundaries have been pushed, is better than allowing a false public narrative to remain dominant. He urged the intelligence community (IC) to continue to think more deeply about these important ethical issues and related issues of data quality.

GAPS IN THE *ANALYTIC FRAMEWORK*

Rebstock pointed out that the *Analytic Framework* could not cover all areas of interest. For example, Charles Lau (co-lead expert contributor for the *Analytic Framework* and director of the International Survey Research Program at RTI International) highlighted the lack of information on the relationship between attitudes and behavior in the *Analytic Framework*. Kennedy added that the academic literature more broadly is lacking in terms of how to deal with sensitive measurements; the scientific community has more work to do to provide better tools to collect those types of measurements.

An analyst asked whether useful information could be collected from a snowball poll of elites across several countries. Bautista suggested using the quality tool in the *Analytic Framework* to try to understand the research process and develop more confidence in the credibility of the information and the soundness of the conclusions that are drawn from it. An analyst would explore the following questions about the data quality before evaluating the conclusions: who sponsored the study? Who was approached to participate in the study? Who conducted the study? Is the survey authentic? Were professional standards followed? The "beauty" of the *Analytic Framework*, he continued, is that it is a portable tool that intelligence analysts can apply to many types of scenarios.

Pasek added that it is important to consider strategies to approach a true black box. If the black box is worth exploring and no other path exists to obtain its data, analysts would need to determine whether they could validate parts of it in enough ways to trust the observations. Amaya noted that black boxes are usually a bad indicator, and black box processes are iterative: once an analyst determines how much validation is possible, the analytic plan might need to be revised. She cautioned against making comparisons across countries with a black box because it is impossible to know what has changed across the countries. She pointed out that black box scenarios and snowball samples (the latter of which is discussed in her chapter in the *Analytic Framework*) are often well suited for qualitative approaches—the data can reveal a theme, which is a "safer" way to use these data and build confidence in them. She suggested that intelligence analysts study everything that could go wrong in these situations, understand the details of the relevant sampling approaches, and use Bautista's rating system to evaluate quality. Lau also emphasized the danger in drawing cross-country inferences using these types of data sources because each country likely has a different sampling approach, recruitment approach, and composition. He commented that these types of sources are better suited to reveal qualitative insights about what is happening within countries.

Because intelligence analysts might be unfamiliar with the approaches presented in the *Analytic Framework*, Bautista proposed that they practice, essentially training themselves until these strategies become part of their everyday thinking. Rebstock requested that the IC provide feedback in the coming months on whether and how the *Analytic Framework* is being used.

REFLECTIONS ON THE *ANALYTIC FRAMEWORK* PROJECT

Elizabeth Zechmeister (co-lead expert contributor for the *Analytic Framework*, and Cornelius Vanderbilt Professor of Political Science and director of the Latin American Public Opinion Project at Vanderbilt University) described the learning process required for academics to better understand the work of intelligence analysts. She remarked that academics have a tendency to look critically at data and focus on the challenges that arise when trying to use a dataset or methodology, a mindset that somewhat contrasts that of intelligence analysts, who have an immediate task to accomplish and prioritize accordingly. Thus, she said that analysts benefit from having quality checklists and menus of options for data collection and inference.

Despite the difference between the academic and policy arenas, Zechmeister continued, the workshop discussions revealed several commonalities between the two communities: (1) a shared commitment to scientific rigor in achieving the best possible estimates of opinion as well as the assessments of certainty around them and their stability; (2) agreement on the importance of normalizing the integration of ethics in empirical research with respect to human subjects, the research team, and potential long-term consequences of research efforts; and (3) a mutual understanding of the challenge of translating survey science to educated nonexperts—more work could be done to identify language and frames that will increase the trust these stakeholders have in the work.

Zechmeister explained that the *Analytic Framework* is intended to be as broadly useful to the IC as possible, reflecting varied levels of dialogue to appeal to analysts with different types of experience and different responsibilities within the IC. She expressed her hope that the *Analytic Framework* provides helpful guidance and resources and encouraged the IC to explore its four commissioned papers in greater detail: (1) "Drawing Inferences from Public Opinion Surveys: Insights for Intelligence Reports," written by Bautista, presents a two-fold rating system to evaluate the quality of a dataset; (2) "Alternatives to Probability-based Surveys Representative of the General Population for Measuring Attitudes," written by Amaya, offers an inventory of different nonprobability sampling approaches as well as a discussion of the advantages and disadvantages of each; (3) "Ascertaining True Attitudes in Survey Research," written by Kanisha Bond (assistant professor of political science at Binghamton University, State University of New York), provides examples of approaches to implicit attitudes and sensitive topics; and (4) "Integrating Data Across Sources," written by Pasek and Sunghee Lee (research associate professor at the Institute for Social Research at the University of Michigan), presents an inventory of methods for data integration (NASEM, 2022). Zechmeister also highlighted several of the practical ideas that surfaced during the workshop, including the use of list experiments and issues of data quality in online research.

Zechmeister reviewed the key themes presented by the *Analytic Framework*, illuminating the importance of

- assessing quality across multiple dimensions;
- planning before conducting analyses (e.g., availability of documentation, design of analysis strategy, and articulation of expectations);
- elevating the role of humans in the research process;
- analyzing metadata to understand how a survey was conducted as part of the ethics and quality checks and to make inferences more sound;
- thinking about culture and its influence on survey response;
- keeping pace with the changing landscape of technology for data collection and analysis (e.g., rolling data collections and experiments, Short Message Service surveys, and online polls);
- pushing at the frontier as a community and continuing to learn from one another; and
- remaining aware of the differences across higher- and lower-capacity or income environments when applying cutting-edge technologies (e.g., the efficacy of a phone survey in a high-income, high-capacity context versus in a multilingual low-income, low-capacity context).

The workshop discussions revealed several challenges to implementing the guidance in the *Analytic Framework*. Zechmeister noted that intelligence analysts often respond to emerging policy questions in reactive situations without time or space to develop a research plan. Furthermore, their incentives are aligned to producing a recommendation to a policy maker who is a generalist. Thus, a dichotomy exists between this reality in which the IC operates on a day-to-day basis and the *Analytic Framework*, which presents a "deep dive" into the foundation of public opinion research. This reinforces the value of the ICs taking time to have the types of discussions that occurred during the workshop, to research and prepare in advance of crisis situations, to develop checklists, and to expand its inventory of data analysis techniques. She applauded the IC for its exceptional work to make the best recommendations with imperfect data. She posited that the *Analytic Framework* is a step toward future action but not the last step, with space to build on its foundation and emphasize "next-generation questions."

Lau expressed his appreciation for the "pressure-testing" of the *Analytic Framework* that occurred throughout the workshop's scenario-based discussions and noted how much he learned about its application. He commended Zachariah Mampilly (expert contributor for the *Analytic Framework* and Marxe Endowed Chair of International Affairs at the Marxe School of Public and International Affairs, City University of New York) for raising questions about ethics early in the experts' discussions and echoed Bond's point that the ethical and technical aspects of survey measurement are intertwined. Lau reiterated that the work of intelligence analysts is very difficult—they are experts in their own right.

A representative from the IC conveyed her gratitude for all of the contributions to the *Analytic Framework* and said that it achieved the IC's three key objectives: (1) What is the state of the art? (2) How can that knowledge be used for decision-making processes in the IC? (3) How can those insights best be combined and communicated to the policy community? The four scenarios discussed during the workshop demonstrated that intelligence analysts can conduct high-quality analyses and continue to defend national security with the resources available in the *Analytic Framework*, which is multilayered with ample citations to other relevant literature.

Rebstock and Barbara Wanchisen (senior advisor for the behavioral sciences in the Division of Behavioral and Social Sciences and Education within the National Academies) observed that the work of the *Analytic Framework* could also be useful for other government agencies. They thanked the IC for its vision and support of the project, as well as all staff, expert panelists, and authors who contributed to the success of the endeavor.

References

ARC (Advancing Conflict Research). (n.d.). *The ARC Bibliography*. https://advancingconflictresearch.com/resources-1.

Arjona, A., Mampilly, Z., and Pearlman, W. (2019). Research in violent or post-conflict political settings. *American Political Science Association Organized Section for Qualitative and Multi-Method Research, Qualitative Transparency Deliberations*. https://papers.ssrn.com/sol3/papers.cfm?abstract_id=3333503.

Berry, J.W. (1969). On cross-cultural comparability. *International Journal of Psychology, 4*, 119–128.

Choi, V.K., Shrestha, S., Pan, X., and Gelfand, M.J. (2022). When danger strikes: A linguistic tool for tracking America's collective response to threats. *Proceedings of the National Academy of Sciences of the United States of America, 119*(4), e2113891119. https://doi.org/10.1073/pnas.2113891119.

Farh, J.-L., Earley, P.C., and Lin, S.-C. (1997). Impetus for action: A cultural analysis of justice and organizational citizenship behavior in Chinese society. *Administrative Science Quarterly, 42*(3), 421–444. https://doi.org/10.2307/2393733.

Gelfand, M.J., Raver, J.L., and Ehrhart, K.H. (2002). Methodological issues in cross-cultural organizational research. In S.G. Rogelberg (Ed.), *Handbook of Research Methods in Industrial and Organizational Psychology* (pp. 216–246). Blackwell Publishing.

Gelfand, M.J., Severance, L., Lee, T., Bruss, C.B., Lun, J., Abdel-Latif, A.-H., Al-Moghazy, A.A., and Ahmed, S.M. (2015). Culture and getting to yes: The linguistic signature of creative agreements in the United States and Egypt. *Journal of Organizational Behavior, 36*(7), 967–989. https://doi.org/10.1002/job.2026.

Hui, C.H., and Triandis, H.C. (1985). Measurement in cross-cultural psychology: A review and comparison of strategies. *Journal of Cross-Cultural Psychology, 16*(2), 131–152. https://doi.org/10.1177/0022002185016002001.

Malpass, R.S. (1977). Theory and method in cross-cultural psychology. *American Psychologist, 32*, 1069–1079.

NASEM (National Academies of Sciences, Engineering, and Medicine). (2022). *Measurement and Analysis of Public Opinion: An Analytic Framework*. Washington, DC: The National Academies Press.

Parker, C. (2022, March 8). 58 percent of Russians support the invasion of Ukraine, and 23 percent oppose it, new poll shows. *Washington Post*. https://www.washingtonpost.com/world/2022/03/08/russia-public-opinion-ukraine-invasion/.

Weber, E.U., Hsee, C.K., and Sokolowska, J. (1998). What folklore tells us about risk and risk taking: Cross-cultural comparisons of American, German, and Chinese proverbs. *Organizational Behavior and Human Decision Processes, 75*(2), 170–186.

Appendix A

Workshop Agenda

MEASUREMENT AND ANALYSIS OF PUBLIC OPINION:
AN ANALYTIC FRAMEWORK
WORKSHOP ON THE ANALYTIC FRAMEWORK
AND ITS APPLICATIONS
MARCH 8–9, 2022

The National Academy of Sciences
Lecture Room and via WebEx
2101 Constitution Avenue NW
Washington, DC 20418

AGENDA

Measuring and analyzing public opinion comes with tremendous challenges, as evidenced by recent struggles to predict election outcomes and to anticipate mass mobilizations. The recent National Academies publication *Measurement and Analysis of Public Opinion: An Analytic Framework* presents in-depth information from experts on how to collect public opinion data and glean insights from such data, particularly in conditions where contextual issues call for applying caveats to public opinion data.

This workshop will briefly present the *Analytic Framework* and demonstrate its application across a series of hypothetical scenarios that might be faced by an intelligence analyst tasked with summarizing public attitudes to inform a policy decision.

Workshop Objectives
- *Provide an overview of the* Analytic Framework's *components: the foundational papers, the synthesis, and the graphic depiction of the phases involved in collecting and analyzing public opinion data*
- *Examine key messages in the* Framework *and discuss what the Framework does and does not do*
- *Explore cultural and ethical considerations in the collection and use of public opinion data*
- *Engage in several exercises applying the* Analytic Framework *to theoretical scenarios and address intelligence analysts' questions about its application*

Tuesday, March 8, 2022 (Please note all times are Eastern Standard Time)

10:00 am EST   **WELCOME**

    Samantha Chao
    Associate Executive Director Extension, National Research Council Programs
    National Academies of Sciences, Engineering, and Medicine

10:10 am   **THE ROLE OF PUBLIC OPINION IN INTELLIGENCE ANALYSIS**

    Regina Faranda
    Director, Office of Opinion Research
    U.S. Department of State

10:20 am   **WORKSHOP GOALS**

    Charles Lau, *Co-Lead Expert Contributor for the Analytic Framework*
    Director, International Survey Research Program
    RTI International

10:35 am   **CHALLENGES ANALYSTS FACE**

    A representative from the Intelligence Community will describe some of the challenges intelligence analysts face to foreground the workshop in their experiences.

10:50 am **OVERVIEW OF THE ANALYTIC FRAMEWORK AND KEY MESSAGES FOR INTELLIGENCE ANALYSTS**

Representative from the Intelligence Community

Charles Lau

Elizabeth Zechmeister, *Co-Lead Expert Contributor for the Analytic Framework*
Cornelius Vanderbilt Professor of Political Science and Director, LAPOP (Latin American Public Opinion Project)
Vanderbilt University

11:35 am **BREAK FOR LUNCH**

1:05 pm **CULTURAL AND ETHICAL CONSIDERATIONS IN THE COLLECTION AND USE OF PUBLIC OPINION DATA**

Ethical Considerations
Zachariah Mampilly, *Expert Contributor for the Analytic Framework*
Marxe Endowed Chair of International Affairs, Marxe School of Public and International Affairs
City University of New York

Kanisha Bond, *Author, Ascertaining True Attitudes in Survey Research*
Assistant Professor of Political Science
Binghamton University (SUNY)

Cultural Considerations
Michele Gelfand, *Expert Contributor for the Analytic Framework*
John H. Scully Professor in Cross-Cultural Management and Professor of Organizational Behavior, Stanford Graduate School of Business
Professor of Psychology (by courtesy), School of Humanities and Sciences
Stanford University

2:20 pm **APPLYING THE *ANALYTIC FRAMEWORK* TO HYPOTHETICAL SCENARIOS**

Charles Lau

In each of the next four sessions, three of the Expert Contributors for the Analytic Framework *that guided its development will describe how they would approach a hypothetical scenario from their academic perspective (30 minutes)*

Following this discussion, a representative from the Intelligence Community will offer initial reactions. (10 minutes

The remainder of each session is reserved for Q&A/ dialog with Intelligence Community audience members. We invite reactions, comments on where more detail is needed, and questions for the Expert Contributors and Foundational Paper authors.

2:25 pm **SCENARIO 1: Evaluating Political Support in a Multi-Ethnic Country**

IC Analyst	Rachel is an early career IC analyst with limited background in survey research.
Country	Multi-ethnic, low-income country
IC analyst task	Rachel is tasked with summarizing the public's attitudes about the prime minister within 5 business days, with a focus on variation by ethnic groups.
Data sources available	Rachel has access to: (1) a high-quality face-to-face survey conducted by the US Department of State two years ago; (2) a well-executed mobile phone survey conducted by US Department of State three months ago; (3) an online poll from last week conducted by the dominant political

party and published on the party's website, with minimal documentation. Individual-level (micro) data are available for (1) and (2) but not (3).

William "Chip" Eveland, *Expert Contributor for the Analytic Framework*
Professor of Communication, Professor of Political Science (by courtesy)
The Ohio State University

Scott E. Page, *Expert Contributor for the Analytic Framework*
John Seely Brown Distinguished University Professor of Complexity, Social Science, and Management
University of Michigan

Elizabeth Zechmeister

Representative from the Intelligence Community

3:25 pm	**WRAP UP DAY ONE**
	Charles Lau
3:35 pm	**ADJOURN DAY ONE**

Wednesday, March 9, 2022

10:00 am	**WELCOME AND OVERVIEW OF DAY TWO**	
	Charles Lau	
10:10 am	**SCENARIO 2: REACTING TO A MILITARY COUP**	
	IC Analyst	Tanya is a mid-level IC analyst with 5 years of experience working surveys
	Country	Middle-income country. This country is an important security partner of the US in a strategic region. The country

	recently experienced a military coup and there are significant security challenges in the northern part of the country. The government has declared a state of emergency, so face-to-face surveys are not feasible.
IC analyst task	Tanya is tasked with developing a plan for how the agency can understand public opinion within 1 month.
Data sources available	Tanya has access to no existing data sources.

D. Sunshine Hillygus, *Expert Contributor for the Analytic Framework*
Professor of Political Science, Professor of Public Policy (by courtesy)
Duke University

Courtney Kennedy, *Expert Contributor for the Analytic Framework*
Director, Survey Research
Pew Research Center

Lisa Mueller, *Expert Contributor for the Analytic Framework*
Associate Professor of Political Science
Macalester College

Representative from the Intelligence Community

11:10 am   **SCENARIO 3: ANTICIPATING POLITICAL INSTABILITY**

IC Analyst	Luis is an early career IC analyst with no background in survey research
Region	Politically unstable *region* (~15 countries) with significant security challenges

APPENDIX A

IC analyst task	Luis is tasked with describing public opinion in the region, with a focus on recommending countries where popular discontent with the regime may emerge in the next year.
Data sources available	20 surveys (5 mobile phone, 5 social media nonprobability web surveys, 10 face-to-face) from the past 5 years. The surveys vary in quality: some follow highest quality standards (micro-data available), some are low-cost/lower-quality surveys (micro-data available), some are poor quality (no micro-data available).

James N. Druckman, *Expert Contributor for the Analytic Framework*
Payson S. Wild Professor of Political Science
Northwestern University

Charles Lau

Representative from the Intelligence Community

12:10 pm	**SCENARIO FOUR SELECTION**
	National Academies Staff
12:30 pm	**BREAK FOR LUNCH**
2:00 pm	**SCENARIO 4: AUDIENCE CHOICE**
	Expert Contributors for the Analytic Framework
	Representative from the Intelligence Community

3:00 pm   **WHAT WE HAVE LEARNED AND FUTURE DIRECTIONS**

Expert Contributors will reflect on the following:

- *What insights have you gained over the course of this workshop?*
- *In light of the workshop discussions, are there additional methods not discussed in depth in the* Analytic Framework *that warrant consideration by intelligence analysts tasked with investigating public opinion?*

3:45 pm   **WRAP-UP/CLOSING REMARKS**

Elizabeth Zechmeister
Charles Lau
Representative from the Intelligence Community

4:15 pm   **ADJOURN WORKSHOP**

Appendix B

Biographical Information for Workshop Participants

INVITED SPEAKER

Regina Faranda is the director of the Office of Opinion Research in the Bureau of Intelligence and Research (INR) and a career member of the Senior Executive Service (SES). Throughout her 20-year tenure in INR, she has been dedicated to informing U.S. policy making by providing a seat at the U.S. policy table for people around the world. Faranda's team of international pollsters are experts on the countries they cover, quantitative social science, and all-source analysis. They conduct analysis of foreign opinion in all regions of the world, provide intelligence support to department principals, and conduct public opinion polls and all-source research to gauge foreign attitudes about influence, governance, international security, trade and economy, ethnic and social relations, democratic transitions, and other issues. Faranda has received six SES-level performance awards. Before her SES tenure, she was INR's "Analyst of the Year" in 2010 and received two Superior Honor and three Meritorious Honor awards, including one for outstanding support to the President's Daily Briefing book. She has expertise on Russia, Ukraine, and Central Asia. She has degrees in history, economics, and Russian from The Ohio State University and Georgetown University, and studied Ukrainian at Harvard University, survey methods at the University of Maryland, and statistics at the Berlin-Brandenburg Academy of Sciences.

EXPERT CONTRIBUTORS FOR THE *ANALYTIC FRAMEWORK*

James N. Druckman (*Planning Committee Member*) is the Payson S. Wild Professor of Political Science and Faculty Fellow at the Institute for Policy Research at Northwestern University. He is also an Honorary Professor of Political Science at Aarhus University in Denmark. His research focuses on political preference formation and communication. His work examines how citizens make political, economic, and social decisions in various contexts (e.g., settings with multiple competing messages, online information, deliberation). He also researches the relationship between citizens' preferences and public policy. Druckman has published roughly 140 articles and book chapters in political science, communication, economic, science, and psychology journals. His latest book is *Experimental Thinking: A Primer for Social Science Experiments* (Cambridge University Press). He has served as editor of the journals *Political Psychology* and *Public Opinion Quarterly* as well as the University of Chicago Press's series in American Politics. He currently is the co-principal investigator of Time-sharing Experiments for the Social Sciences. He is an elected member of the American Academy of Arts and Sciences, and the recipient of a John Simon Guggenheim Memorial Foundation Fellowship. He holds a Ph.D. in political science from the University of California, San Diego, and a B.A. from Northwestern University, majoring in mathematical methods in the social sciences and political science.

William "Chip" Eveland, Jr. is professor of communication and (by courtesy) political science at The Ohio State University (2000–present). Prior to his arrival at Ohio State, Eveland was an assistant professor of communication (1998–2000) and founding director of a survey research center at the University of California, Santa Barbara. He also has worked in a research role for the National Institute for Science Education (2006–2008) evaluating online science communication efforts. Eveland's academic research focuses on the role of political communication in developing informed and participatory citizens of democracy, both in the United States and also, increasingly, around the globe. Although his early research focused on the effects of news media use on political knowledge and participation, more recently his work has highlighted the important role of the structure and content of political discussion networks in democracy. Eveland's most recent work emphasizes the important role of "listening" in political conversations where there are deep divides, not only due to partisanship but also across lines of racial difference and about race-related topics. Eveland has published in the fields of communication, political science, sociology, and psychology, and much of that published work has centered on empirical evaluation of the accuracy of survey measurement of concepts such as news media use, political conversation, and political knowledge.

Michele Gelfand (NAS) is professor of organizational behavior at the Stanford Graduate School of Business and professor of psychology by courtesy at Stanford University. She studies the evolution of culture and its multilevel consequences for human groups. Her work has been cited more than 40,000 times and has been featured in such outlets as the *Washington Post*, the *New York Times*, National Public Radio, Voice of America, and *The Economist*. Gelfand has published in numerous premier journals, including *Science*, the *Proceedings of the National Academy of Sciences*, *Psychological Science*, *Nature Scientific Reports*, and *American Psychologist*. She is the founding co-editor of the *Advances in Culture and Psychology Annual Series* and the *Frontiers of Culture and Psychology* series. Gelfand is the past president of the International Association for Conflict Management and past division chair of the Conflict Division of the Academy of Management. She received the 2017 Outstanding International Psychologist Award from the American Psychological Association, the 2016 Diener award from the Society for Personality and Social Psychology, and the Annaliese Research Award from the Alexander von Humboldt Foundation. Her work published in *Science* was honored with the Gordon Allport Intergroup Relations Prize from the Society for the Psychological Study of Social Issues. She is the author of *Rule Makers, Rule Breakers: How Tight and Loose Cultures Wire the World* (2018, Scribner). She obtained a B.A. in psychology from the Colgate University and a Ph.D. in social psychology and organizational psychology from the University of Illinois, Urbana-Champaign.

D. Sunshine Hillygus is professor of political science and public policy and founding director of the Initiative on Survey Methodology at Duke University. Her research on public opinion and survey methodology has been funded by the National Science Foundation and published in dozens of academic journal articles. She is co-author of *Making Young Voters: Converting Civic Attitudes into Civic Action* (Cambridge University Press, 2020), *The Persuadable Voter: Wedge Issues in Political Campaigns* (Princeton University Press, 2008), and *The Hard Count: The Social and Political Challenges of the 2000 Census* (Russell Sage Foundation, 2006). She served on the Census Scientific Advisory Committee from 2012 to 2018 and is currently a member of the American Statistical Association Taskforce on 2020 Census Quality Indicators and the American Association of Public Opinion Research Taskforce on 2020 Election Polling Performance. She is associate principal investigator of the 2020 American National Election Study and associate editor of *Political Analysis*. From 2003 to 2009, she taught at Harvard University, where she was the Frederick S. Danziger Associate Professor of Government and founding director of the Program on Survey Research. She holds a Ph.D. in political science from Stanford University and a B.A. from the University of Arkansas.

Michael Hout (NAS) is professor of sociology at New York University. He uses demographic methods to study social change in inequality, religion, and politics. He was co-principal investigator on the General Social Survey (GSS) from 2008 to 2016, and currently uses the GSS to study changing occupational hierarchies, social mobility, and social attitudes since 1972. He chairs the National Academies' Advisory Committee for the Division of Behavioral and Social Sciences and Education, and has served on the Societal Experts Action Network, Committee on National Statistics, Steering Committee for a Workshop on Developing a New National Survey on Social Mobility, and the Board on Testing and Assessment. Hout's books include *Century of Difference* (with Claude Fischer, 2006), *The Truth about Conservative Christians* (with Andrew Greeley, 2006), *Inequality by Design* (with five Berkeley colleagues, 1996), *Following in Father's Footsteps: Social Mobility in Ireland* (1989), and *Mobility Tables* (1983). Illustrative papers include "Americans' Occupational Status Reflects the Status of Both of Their Parents" (2018); "Social and Economic Returns to Higher Education in the United States" (2012); and "Race, Immigration, and Political Polarization" (with Maggio, 2021). He was elected to the American Academy of Arts & Sciences in 1997, the National Academy of Sciences in 2003, and the American Philosophical Society in 2006. He received a B.A. from the University of Pittsburgh in history and sociology and an M.A. and a Ph.D. from Indiana University in sociology.

Courtney Kennedy (*Planning Committee Member*) is director of survey research at Pew Research Center. In this role, she serves as the chief survey methodologist for the Center, providing guidance on all of its research and leading its methodology work. Prior to joining Pew Research Center, Kennedy served as vice president of the advanced methods group at Abt SRBI, where she was responsible for designing complex surveys, developing data collection methodologies, and assessing data quality. Her work has been published in *Public Opinion Quarterly*, the *Journal of Survey Statistics and Methodology*, and the *Journal of Official Statistics*. She has worked as a statistical consultant on the U.S. Census Bureau's decennial census and on multiple reports appearing in *Newsweek*. Kennedy has served as standards chair and conference chair of the American Association for Public Opinion Research. She holds a Ph.D. from the University of Michigan and an M.A. from the University of Maryland, both in survey methodology.

Charles Lau (*Planning Committee Chair*) is director of the International Survey Research Program at RTI International, where he specializes in survey methodology and implementation in low- and middle-income countries. Lau has led surveys in more than 30 countries. He directs projects throughout the survey cycle, including study design, questionnaire development, sampling, interviewer training, data collection, analysis, and reporting. In partnership with government, foundation, and commercial clients, his work has covered various topics including public health; politics, security, and conflict; technology; and economic growth and education. Across topics, Lau develops innovative methods to improve measurement quality and enhance the quality of survey sampling. His recent areas of focus include using geographic information systems for household survey sampling and pioneering methodological best practices for mobile phone surveys in low- and middle-income countries. Lau publishes methodological research on cross-cultural issues in questionnaire design, interviewer and mode effects, and sampling approaches in developing countries. His research has appeared in journals such as *International Journal of Public Opinion Research*, *Survey Research Methods*, the *Journal of International Development*. He holds a Ph.D. in sociology and an M.S. in epidemiology from the University of California, Los Angeles, and a B.A. in sociology from Brown University.

Zachariah Mampilly is the Marxe Endowed Chair of International Affairs at the Marxe School of Public and International Affairs, City University of New York. In 2012–2013, he was a Fulbright Visiting Professor at the University of Dar es Salaam, Tanzania. He has lived, worked, and studied in Africa, South Asia, and North America. An expert on the politics of both violent and nonviolent resistance, he is the author of *Rebel Rulers: Insurgent Governance and Civilian Life during War* (Cornell University Press 2011), based on extensive fieldwork in rebel-controlled zones of Congo, Sri Lanka, and South Sudan. *Africa Uprising: Popular Protest and Political Change* (Zed Press, 2015), co-written with Adam Branch, examines the ongoing Third Wave of African protest and provides an inside look at recent movements in Ethiopia, Nigeria, Uganda, and Sudan. Mampilly writes widely on South Asian and African politics for a variety of publications, including *Al Jazeera*, *The Hindu*, *The Washington Post*, *Foreign Affairs*, and *N+1*. Mampilly teaches courses on civil wars and rebel movements; race, ethnicity, and nationalism; and the international relations of the Third World. He holds a Ph.D. from the University of California, Los Angeles, an M.A. from Columbia University, and a B.A. from Tufts University.

Lisa Mueller is associate professor of political science and the director of African Studies at Macalester College. Her book, *Political Protest in Contemporary Africa* (Cambridge University Press), received an honorable mention from the African Politics Conference Group for Best Book of 2018. Mueller's other work has appeared in leading journals, including *Electoral Studies*, *African Affairs*, and the *African Studies Review*. She is a frequent contributor to the "Monkey Cage" blog of the *Washington Post* and an advisor to United States Agency for International Development, the State Department, the World Bank, and other governmental and nongovernmental agencies. She has conducted fieldwork in Niger, Senegal, Mali, Guinea, Burkina Faso, Malawi, and Mauritius. She received her B.A. from Pomona College and her master's degree and Ph.D. from the University of California, Los Angeles, specializing in comparative politics, political economy, social movements, and research methods.

Diana C. Mutz holds the Samuel A. Stouffer Chair in Political Science and Communication at the University of Pennsylvania where she also serves as director of the Institute for the Study of Citizens and Politics. She has published numerous articles on public opinion, political psychology, and the media in a wide variety of academic journals. Her award-winning books include *Winners and Losers: The Psychology of Foreign Trade* (Princeton, 2021), *In-Your-Face Politics: The Consequences of Uncivil Media* (Princeton, 2015), *The Obama Effect: How the 2008 Campaign Changed White Racial Attitudes* (Russell Sage Foundation, 2014), *Population-Based Survey Experiments* (Princeton, 2011), *Hearing the Other Side: Deliberative Versus Participatory Democracy* (Cambridge, 2006), and *Impersonal Influence* (Cambridge, 1998). Mutz was inducted as a fellow of the American Academy of Arts and Sciences in 2008. In 2011, Mutz received the Lifetime Career Achievement Award in Political Communication from the American Political Science Association. She received a Guggenheim Fellowship in 2015, and a Carnegie Foundation Fellowship in 2016 to study the impact of globalization on American public opinion. She was founding co-principal investigator of Time-sharing Experiments for the Social Sciences, an infrastructure project supporting innovative methodology across the social sciences. She holds a Ph.D. in communications from Stanford University and a B.S. from Northwestern University.

Scott E. Page (*Planning Committee Member*) is the John Seely Brown Distinguished University Professor of Complexity, Social Science, and Management at the University of Michigan. He is also the Williamson Family Professor of Business Administration; professor of management and organizations, Stephen M. Ross School of Business; and professor of political science, professor of complex systems, and professor of economics, College of Literature, Science, and the Arts. Page is also an external faculty member of the Santa Fe Institute. His research focuses on the function of diversity in complex social systems, the potential for collective intelligence, and the design of institutions for meeting the challenges of a complex world. A recipient of a Guggenheim Fellowship, a fellowship at the Center for Advanced Studies in the Behavioral Sciences at Stanford, Page was elected a fellow of the American Academy of Arts and Sciences in 2011. His fifth book, *The Model Thinker*, was published by Basic Books in November 2018. He has been a featured speaker at The World Economic Forum–Davos, *The New York Times* New Work Summit, Google Re:Work, and The Aspen Ideas Festival and has consulted with the Federal Reserve System, the White House Office of Personnel, Yahoo!, Ford, the Defense Advanced Research Projects Agency, Procter and Gamble, BlackRock, and AB InBev. He holds a Ph.D. in managerial economics and decision sciences from Northwestern University, an M.A. in mathematics from the University of Wisconsin, and an A.B. from the University of Michigan in mathematics.

Elizabeth J. Zechmeister is Cornelius Vanderbilt Professor of Political Science and director of the Latin American Public Opinion Project (LAPOP) Lab at Vanderbilt University. Her research expertise is in public opinion, political behavior, and research methodology. She has published more than 30 articles and two books: *Democracy at Risk: How Terrorist Threats Affect the Public* (University of Chicago Press, 2009) and *Latin American Party Systems* (Cambridge Press, 2010). She is co-editor of *The Latin American Voter* (University of Michigan Press, 2015). Her research on public opinion in times of crisis has been awarded multiple grants from the U.S. National Science Foundation. In her work as LAPOP director, she leads the AmericasBarometer—a regular regional survey of democracy and public opinion in 34 countries. She is the current chair of the global Comparative Study of Electoral Systems project, and serves on several journal editorial boards as well as several advisory boards in the area of public opinion research and methodology. Zechmeister has received Vanderbilt's Jeffrey Nordhaus Award for Excellence in Undergraduate Teaching and Vanderbilt's Award for Excellence in Graduate Teaching. She is an experienced public speaker, who has given dozens of talks on public opinion and survey methodology to academic and nonacademic audiences. She holds a Ph.D. in political science from Duke University and an M.A. from the University of Chicago, majoring in Latin American studies.

INTELLIGENCE COMMUNITY

Participants in this workshop include analysts and managers from the intelligence community (IC), each of whom is seeking to help IC analysts consistently draw from the most recent advances in the social and behavioral sciences to make sense of information about the world. Most have graduate degrees from major U.S. institutions, in disciplines such as economics, psychology, political psychology, political science, sociology, and statistics.

AUTHORS

Ashley Amaya (author, "Alternatives to Probability-based Surveys Representative of the General Population for Measuring Attitudes") is a senior survey methodologist at Pew Research Center. In this role, she serves as an advisor for projects involving address-based sampling, multiple modes of data collection, and surveys of rare populations. Amaya's work on address-based sampling methods, Web panel surveys, and the use of alternative data sources to replace and enhance survey data has been published in a variety of journals, including *Public Opinion Quarterly*, *Journal of Survey Statistics and Methods*, and *Social Science Computer Review*. Prior to joining Pew Research Center, she was a senior survey methodologist at RTI International, where she led research into address-based sampling methods and applications. She has served as editor-in-chief of *Survey Practice*, chair of the short course subcommittee for the American Association for Public Opinion Research (AAPOR), membership chair of the DC-Baltimore chapter of AAPOR, and communications chair of the Washington Statistical Society. She has a Ph.D. from the University of Maryland and a master's degree from the University of Michigan, both in survey methodology. She received her bachelor's degree from the University of Michigan.

René Bautista (author, "Drawing Inferences from Public Opinion Surveys: Insights for Intelligence Reports") is the associate director of the Methodology and Quantitative Social Sciences department at NORC at the University of Chicago, where he has worked since 2010. He is also the director and co-principal investigator of the General Social Survey, one of the most influential social science surveys monitoring societal change. Bautista has substantial experience with survey research designs, qualitative work, and advanced statistical analysis. His academic research focuses on nonresponse, measurement error, interviewer effects, mixed modes, cross-cultural research, and data collection methods. He is a frequent presenter in national and international survey methods conferences hosted by major professional organizations, where he is an active member. Bautista has served as executive councilor of the American Association for Public Opinion Research (AAPOR), chairing the Standards Committee. Bautista has also served as associate editor of *Public Opinion Quarterly*—the premier scholarly publication of AAPOR. He is currently an executive committee member of the European Survey Research Association. He is also a member of other major organizations, including the World Association for Public Opinion and the American Statistical Association. Bautista serves as a reviewer for leading national and international journals in public opinion, survey statistics, and research methodology, and teaches Survey Questionnaire Design courses at the Irving B. Harris Graduate School of Public Policy Studies at the

University of Chicago. He holds a Ph.D. in survey research and methodology from the University of Nebraska-Lincoln.

Kanisha D. Bond (author, "Ascertaining True Attitudes in Survey Research") is an assistant professor of political science at Binghamton University (State University of New York). She studies culture, violence, and contentious political mobilization, with a special focus on how ideology, race, and gender influence institution-building among radical groups in polarized societies. Her scholarship has been published by the *American Political Science Review*, *Journal of Politics*, *British Journal of Political Science*, *International Negotiation*, *Political Science Research and Methods*, *Qualitative and Mixed Methods Research*, and the Comparative Politics Section of the American Political Science Association. Her writings on the politics of (studying) radical mobilization can also be found in *Foreign Policy*, in the *Washington Post's* Monkey Cage blog, and through the Social Science Research Council. Prior to joining academia, Bond held professional positions with The Urban Institute, the Organization of American States, the Council on Hemispheric Affairs, and Cesar Chavez Public Charter School for Public Policy, all in Washington, DC. Bond earned her Ph.D. in political science from Penn State University in 2010, an M.P.P. in international development and crime policy from Georgetown University, and a B.A. in international relations and Spanish from Bucknell University.

Rona Briere (author, "Synthesis: Using Public Opinion Research to Answer an Intelligence Question") has been working for the National Academies of Sciences, Engineering, and Medicine as an independent contractor since 1980, serving as a writer/editor for the Division of Behavioral and Social Sciences and Education, the Health and Medicine Division (formerly the Institute of Medicine), Policy and Global Affairs, and the Transportation Research Board. During that time, she also has taught a series of report writing courses for National Academies staff. She holds a B.A. from Syracuse University and an M.A., A.B.D., from The Johns Hopkins University.

Sunghee Lee (co-author, "Integrating Data Across Sources") is a research associate professor at the Institute for Social Research at the University of Michigan. She holds a Ph.D. in survey methodology from the Joint Program in Survey Methodology at the University of Maryland. She has extensive experience with survey sampling and methodology for population-based research, having worked on sampling and postsurvey weighting adjustments for various large- and small-scale surveys, including longitudinal surveys and nonprobability sample surveys. These experiences are motivated by her primary research interest: sampling and measurement issues in data collection with linguistic and racial minorities as well as hard-to-reach populations and cross-cultural survey methodology. She currently leads sampling activities for the Health and Retirement Study, a flagship aging study around the world, and provides consultation on methodological approaches for that study. She is also currently leading an extensive portfolio of methodological research on applications of respondent-driven sampling in the recruitment of hard-to-reach populations and measurement noncomparability issues with racial, linguistic, and ethnic minority groups, which collectively demonstrates her focus on the importance of inclusiveness in research methodology.

Josh Pasek (co-author, "Integrating Data Across Sources") is associate professor of communication and media and political science, faculty associate in the Center for Political Studies, and core faculty for the Michigan Institute for Data Science at the University of Michigan. His research explores how new media and psychological processes each shape political attitudes, public opinion, and political behaviors. Pasek also examines issues in the measurement of public opinion including techniques for reducing measurement error and improving population inferences. Current research explores how both accurate and inaccurate political information might influence public opinion and voter decision making; evaluates whether the use of online social networking sites such as Facebook and Twitter might be changing the political information environment; and assesses the conditions under which nonprobability samples, such as those obtained from big data methods or samples of Internet volunteers, can lead to conclusions similar to those of traditional probability samples. His work has been published in *Public Opinion Quarterly*, *Political Communication*, *Communication Research*, and the *Journal of Communication* among other outlets. He also maintains two R packages for producing survey weights (anesrake) and analyzing weighted survey data (weights).

NATIONAL ACADEMIES STAFF

Samantha Chao is associate executive director extension, National Research Council (NRC) Programs. She is responsible for supporting division executive offices in planning and operational activities, serving as a resource for staff on policies and procedures, and directing and coordinating specific programs in these divisions. Chao previously served as acting director of programs for the National Academy of Medicine (NAM) from December 2020 to October 2021. In this role, she oversaw NAM's programs and the program staff teams to ensure they had maximum success and impact, helped relaunch the Global Roadmap for Healthy Longevity, oversaw the strategic planning process for phase two of the Clinician Well-Being Action

Collaborative, and helped plan and fundraise for the next phase of the Committee on Emerging Science, Technology, and Innovation as it moves to a consensus study. Prior to her position at NAM, Chao served as assistant executive officer in the National Research Council (NRC) Executive Office, where she supported the operations of the Governing Board and Governing Board Executive Committee and a wide range of special initiatives. She also played a central role in the development of the NRC's first Strategic Plan. Previously she was a manager at The Pew Charitable Trusts where she developed and implemented a process to ensure the integrity and quality of research produced by teams across almost 30 policy areas. In that role, she advised teams on the design and conduct of high-quality research methods at the national, state, and local levels. At Pew she also worked on the State Health Care Spending project to enumerate the cost of health care to states. She completed an M.P.H. in health policy with a concentration in management at the University of Michigan.

Jacqueline Cole is a senior program assistant with the Board on Behavioral, Cognitive, and Sensory Sciences. She was the lead administrative support assistant for the *Analytic Framework* project funded by the Office of the Director of National Intelligence and has supported several projects funded by the National Institutes of Health. Prior to her position at the National Academies, she worked for The GW Medical Faculty Associates as the residency program administrator for the George Washington University Internal Medicine Residency Programs and as the coordinator for the Underserved Medicine & Public Health Concentration, designed for residents interested in careers in public health and serving the underserved. Prior to her position as the residency program administrator, she worked as the assistant to the founder and president of the Rodham Institute where she coordinated the first annual summit to promote health equity in Washington, DC. She also worked as the lead administrative assistant for the Armed Forces DNA Identification Laboratory, a forensics laboratory specializing in DNA profiling run by the United States Armed Forces. Cole is an avid volunteer and gives her time to organizations working on behalf of the underserved populations and the homeless.

Emma Fine is an associate program officer primarily working on the Board on Health Sciences Policy and has worked at the National Academies for 4.5 years. She currently supports research on the rapidly evolving COVID-19 pandemic. Previously, she staffed a project on the Board on Global Health assessing morbidity and mortality from HIV/AIDS in Rwanda. She also worked on the Board on Behavioral, Cognitive, and Sensory Sciences, where she helped bridge the gap between academic experts and intelligence analysts for the Office of the Director of National Intelligence. Prior to joining the

National Academies, Ms. Fine interned for the U.S. Department of Health and Human Services in the Office of the Assistant Secretary for Preparedness and Response, where she contributed research to the National Health Security Strategy Implementation Plan as well as the intersection between terrorism and public health preparedness. In 2016, Fine graduated from the University of California, Berkeley, where she earned her B.A. in public health and public policy. She is particularly interested in the nexus between public health, intelligence, and national security and she plans to pursue a degree in national security and enter the field of intelligence.

Dylan Thomas Rebstock is a program officer with the Division of Behavioral and Social Sciences and Education focusing on behavioral/social sciences and national security. He was previously the chief of operations for the Latin America Division at the National Security Agency (NSA), where he was responsible for directing the signals intelligence response to security crises in the Western Hemisphere. Additionally, while at NSA, Rebstock served in offices focusing on counterterrorism, counterintelligence, transnational organized crime, and the Middle East, including two interagency field deployments to Afghanistan and Peru. Before getting into national security, Rebstock worked at two DC think tanks focusing on international relations and was involved in local politics, running campaigns in Texas and Georgia. He holds a B.A. in history and government from the University of Texas at Austin and a M.A. in public and international affairs from the University of Pittsburgh.

Barbara A. Wanchisen serves as senior advisor for the behavioral sciences in the Division of Behavioral and Social Sciences and Education within the National Academies of Sciences, Engineering, and Medicine. She is a long-standing member of the Psychonomic Society, American Association for the Advancement of Science (Fellow, Class of 2020), American Psychological Association (Fellow, Division 25), and the Association for Psychological Science. Wanchisen arrived in Washington, DC, to serve as the executive director of the Federation of Behavioral, Psychological, & Cognitive Sciences, a nonprofit advocacy organization. Previous to that role, Wanchisen was professor (tenured) in the Department of Psychology and director of the collegewide Honors Program at Baldwin-Wallace University near Cleveland, Ohio. She received a B.A. in English and philosophy from Bloomsburg University, an M.A. in English from Villanova University, and a Ph.D. in experimental psychology from Temple University.

Tina M. Winters is an associate program officer with the Board on Behavioral, Cognitive, and Sensory Sciences (BBCSS) at the National Academies of Sciences, Engineering, and Medicine. She has worked on a variety of activities within BBCSS on topics including factors that bear on the quality and success of scientific research, behavioral influences on aging, assessing performance for military accession, factors that affect the performance of small units in military environments, program evaluation, and learning across the lifespan. Prior to joining BBCSS in 2011, her work at the National Academies centered on studies and other activities related to K–16 science and mathematics education, educational assessment, and education research. She was a co-editor for the National Academies consensus report *Advancing Scientific Research in Education* and has worked on many other National Academies reports, including *Reducing the Impact of Dementia in America: A Decadal Survey of the Behavioral and Social Sciences*; *Reproducibility and Replicability in Science*; *How People Learn II: Learners, Contexts, and Cultures*; *Enhancing the Effectiveness of Team Science*; *Using Science as Evidence in Public Policy*; *Strengthening Peer Review in Federal Agencies That Support Education Research*; *Scientific Research in Education*; and *Knowing What Students Know: The Science and Design of Educational Assessment*.